THE OFFICIAL 2021/22 YEARBOOK

SEAGULLS

10

BRIGHTON & HOVE ALBION

YEARS AT THE AMEX

AMERICAN EXPRESS

CONTRIBUTORS:
Peter Rogers and Luke Nicoli

A TWOCAN PUBLICATION

©2021. Published by twocan under licence from Brighton & Hove Albion FC.

ISBN: 978-1-914588-07-5

PICTURE CREDITS:
Brighton and Hove Albion FC,
Paul Hazlewood, Action Images,
Alamy and Press Association.

CONTENTS

2021

AUGUST 2021

Saturday	14	Burnley	A	
Saturday	21	Watford	H	
Tuesday	24	Cardiff City	A	EFL Cup 2
Saturday	28	Everton	H	

SEPTEMBER 2021

Saturday	11	Brentford	A	
Sunday	19	Leicester City	H	
Wednesday	22	Swansea City	H	EFL Cup 3
Monday	27	Crystal Palace	A	

OCTOBER 2021

Saturday	2	Arsenal	H	
Saturday	16	Norwich City	A	
Saturday	23	Manchester City	H	
Wednesday	27	Leicester City	A	EFL Cup 4

NOVEMBER 2021

Saturday	6	Newcastle United	H	
Saturday	20	Aston Villa	A	
Saturday	27	Leeds United	H	
Tuesday	30	West Ham United	A	

DECEMBER 2021

Saturday	4	Southampton	A	
Saturday	11	Tottenham Hotspur	H	
Tuesday	14	Wolverhampton Wanderers	H	
Saturday	18	Manchester United	A	
W/C	20			EFL Cup QF
Sunday	26	Brentford	H	
Tuesday	28	Chelsea	A	

2021/22 FIXTURES

2022

JANUARY 2022

Saturday	1	Everton	A
W/C	3		EFL Cup SF1
Saturday	8		FA Cup 3
W/C	10		EFL Cup SF2
Saturday	**15**	**Crystal Palace**	**H**
Saturday	22	Leicester City	A

FEBRUARY 2022

Saturday	5		FA Cup 4
Tuesday	**8**	**Chelsea**	**H**
Saturday	12	Watford	A
Saturday	**19**	**Burnley**	**H**
Saturday	**26**	**Aston Villa**	**H**
Sunday	27		EFL Cup Final

MARCH 2022

Wednesday	2		FA Cup 5
Saturday	5	Newcastle United	A
Saturday	**12**	**Liverpool**	**H**
Saturday	19	Manchester City	A	FA Cup QF

APRIL 2022

Saturday	**2**	**Norwich City**	**H**
Saturday	9	Arsenal	A
Saturday	16	Tottenham Hotspur	A	FA Cup SF
Saturday	**23**	**Southampton**	**H**
Saturday	30	Wolverhampton Wanderers	A

MAY 2022

Saturday	**7**	**Manchester United**	H
Saturday	14		FA Cup Final
Sunday	15	Leeds United	A
Sunday	**22**	**West Ham United**	**H**

BRIGHTON &

EXPRESS
OTBALL
ANCE CENTRE

HOVE ALBION

BACK ROW L-R: Taylor Richards, Jakub Moder, Danny Welbeck, Adam Webster, Shane Duffy, Dan Burn, Lewis Dunk, Joel Veltman, Jurgen Locadia, Pascal Gross.

MIDDLE ROW: Haydon Roberts, Tudor Baluta, Aaron Connolly, Solly March, Robert Sanchez, Kjell Scherpen, Jason Steele, Enock Mwepu, Adam Lallana, Yves Bissouma.

FRONT ROW: Bruno Saltor, Marc Cucurella, Tariq Lamptey, Neal Maupay, Bjorn Hamberg, Graham Potter, Billy Reid, Leandro Trossard, Alexis Mac Allister, Steven Alzate, Ben Roberts.

9

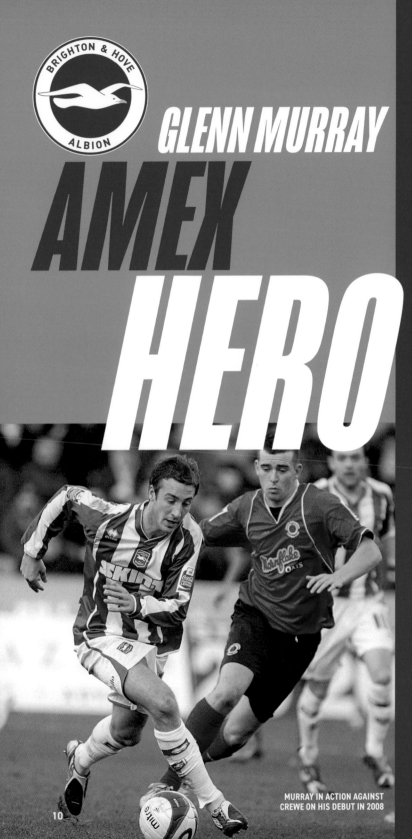

GLENN MURRAY
AMEX HERO

A Brighton & Hove Albion goalscoring sensation from the modern era, striker Glenn Murray netted 111 goals in all competitions across two memorable spells with the Seagulls.

Already viewed as an Amex legend, Murray almost ended up overhauling record goalscorer Tommy Cook's Albion goal tally. Cook netted 123 goals for the club, leaving Murray just 12 goals shy of equalling that record which was set back in the 1920s.

Across his two spells with the club, ace-marksman Murray enjoyed two promotion-winning campaigns with the Seagulls. He first joined the club in January 2008 in a reported £300,000 transfer from Rochdale and marked his home debut with a brace in a 3-0 victory over Crewe Alexandra at Withdean.

Murray's goals proved an essential factor in the team's 2010/11 League One title-winning campaign. He hammered home 22 goals as the Seagulls bade farewell to Withdean and ensured they would begin life at the new Amex Stadium competing at Championship level.

His impressive goals-to-game ratio over a three-and-a-half season period with Albion alerted a number of interested suitors and with his contract coming to an end, he opted to try his luck with arch-rivals Crystal Palace in the summer of 2011. A loan move to Reading and a permanent transfer to AFC Bournemouth then preceded his return to Brighton.

Murray initially rejoined the Seagulls on a season-long loan deal from the Cherries in the summer of 2016 and marked his first appearance as an Albion player at the Amex with a brace in the 3-0 defeat of Nottingham Forest.. He was swiftly right back amongst the goals as Albion worked their way up the Championship table under the management of Chris Hughton. After netting a hat-trick in the 5-0 demolition of Norwich City on 29 October, Murray had certainly won back the hearts of the Albion faithful despite his earlier move to Palace.

With 15 goals in 28 appearances while on loan, the club acted to make the move a permanent one in January 2017 and Murray agreed a deal until the summer of 2019. As a full-time Albion player again, he then scored eight more Championship goals including the first in a historic 2-1 win over Wigan Athletic at the Amex that ultimately proved enough to secure the club promotion to the Premier League.

A dozen Premier League goals followed in 2017/18 and were a major contributing factor in helping Albion secure another season of top-flight football at the Amex.

Murray fired home his 100th league goal for the club in the Seagulls' memorable 2-1 victory over Palace on Saturday 9 March 2019 and from the fans' perspective, he could not have picked a sweeter moment to reach that century landmark.

His final goal in Albion colours came in the thrilling 3-3 draw away to West Ham in February 2020 before he joined Watford on loan and then ended his career playing alongside his former Amex boss, Hughton at Nottingham Forest.

MURRAY IN ACTION AGAINST CREWE ON HIS DEBUT IN 2008

MURRAY NETS HIS 100TH SEAGULLS GOAL V PALACE
IN THE 2-1 VICTORY AT SELHURST PARK, MARCH 2019

FULL NAME:	Glenn Murray
DATE OF BIRTH:	25 September 1983
PLACE OF BIRTH:	Maryport
POSITION:	Striker

SEAGULLS APPEARANCES	SEAGULLS GOALS
287	**111**

LEAGUE:	259	LEAGUE:	103
FA CUP:	19	FA CUP:	6
LEAGUE CUP:	6	LEAGUE CUP:	2
OTHER:	3	OTHER:	0

ALBION DEBUT:	Northampton Town 1-0 Brighton & Hove Albion 29 January 2008 · League One
ALBION HONOURS:	League One title winner 2010/11 Championship runner-up 2016/17

MURRAY SALUTES THE CROWD AFTER SCORING HIS LAST GOAL FOR THE SEAGULLS

After winning promotion back to the second tier as League One champions in 2010/11, there was certainly a feel-good factor both on and off the pitch as the Seagulls began life at the Amex Stadium in the summer of 2011.

Tottenham Hotspur provided the opposition in a pre-season friendly for the official opening of the state-of-the-art stadium on 30 July 2011. The high-profile visitors ran out 3-2 winners, but the result mattered little to the Brighton supporters who were just thrilled to be inside the Albion's new ground. It was an emotional occasion for fans, particularly those who had been forced to leave their spiritual home of the Goldstone Ground back in 1997, travelled to Gillingham and then played the waiting game at Withdean. Finally they now had a place to call 'home' again – and what a home it is!

In something of a twist of fate, it was Doncaster Rovers who provided the first competitive opposition at the new stadium as Championship action got underway. Rovers had of course been the final team to visit the Goldstone back in 1997.

Fittingly for the first league match at the new stadium, it was one of the team's new boys, Will Buckley – a £1m summer signing from Watford – who took the mantle of scoring the club's first competitive goal at their new home. Trailing 1-0 to a 39th-minute Billy Sharp goal, Buckley levelled seven minutes from time and after enjoying the experience so much he did it again in the seventh minute of injury time to spark mass celebrations as Albion marked their return to the second tier with an opening-day victory.

Under the guidance of Gus Poyet, the Seagulls enjoyed an impressive start to the season winning five of their opening six Championship fixtures.

Playing home matches in front of 20,000-plus supporters on a consistent basis certainly showed the true potential of the club. The players rose to the occasion and recorded an impressive tenth-place finish.

Cup competitions provided entertainment and excitement in equal measure too. After defeating Gillingham and Premier League Sunderland at home in the League Cup, Brighton bowed out of the competition to eventual winners Liverpool who marked their first visit to the Amex with a 2-1 win in September 2011.

Ironically it was Liverpool who also called time on Albion's FA Cup adventure. The Seagulls were pushed all the way by Wrexham in the third round – eventually securing a place in the fourth round after a penalty shootout success in the replay. A memorable 1-0 victory over Premier League Newcastle United at the Amex in round four teed up a fifth round meeting with Liverpool at Anfield. The trip to Merseyside saw memories of 1983 flooding back, but on this occasion Albion were no match for a rampant Liverpool.

WILL BUCKLEY'S INJURY-TIME WINNER

BRIGHTON & HOVE ALBION

10

YEARS AT THE AMEX

2011/12

MARCOS PAINTER CONGRATULATES BUCKLEY ON HIS FIRST

MANAGER: *Gus Poyet*
LEAGUE: *Championship*
FINAL LEAGUE POSITION: *10th*
TOP SCORER: *Ashley Barnes (14 IN ALL COMPETITIONS*
LEAGUE WINS: *17*
LEAGUE GOALS SCORED: *52*
LEAGUE POINTS WON: *66*
AVERAGE HOME ATTENDANCE: *20,055*
PLAYER OF THE SEASON: *Liam Bridcutt*

LEONARDO ULLOA CELEBRATES SCORING THE FIRST IN THE 4-1 WIN OVER HUDDERSFIELD, MARCH 2013

MATTHEW UPSON

2012/13

MANAGER: *Gus Poyet*

LEAGUE: *Championship*

FINAL LEAGUE POSITION: **4th**

TOP SCORER: *Craig Mackail-Smith*
(11 IN ALL COMPETITIONS)

LEAGUE WINS: **19**

LEAGUE GOALS SCORED: **69**

LEAGUE POINTS WON: **75**

AVERAGE HOME ATTENDANCE: **26,236**

PLAYER OF THE SEASON: *Liam Bridcutt*

With a first season back in the Championship under their belts, likewise a year settled into their new surrounds at the Amex, all eyes were on the Albion to see if they could mount a sustained Play-Off push in 2012/13.

The side had been greatly strengthened with the likes of Tomasz Kuszczak, Bruno, Wayne Bridge, Andrew Crofts, Dean Hammond and Andrea Orlandi, all arriving at the club during the summer.

The campaign did not get off to the best of starts, with a 1-0 defeat at Hull City, followed by a 0-0 home draw against Cardiff City, but five successive wins soon got the team back on track. The sequence included eye-catching home wins against Barnsley [5-1] and Sheffield Wednesday [3-0], which lifted the side to the top of the table in September while laying down a marker for what was to come.

The FA Cup again brought a buzz to the city with Newcastle United succumbing to a shock defeat for a second successive season – with the reward being the visit of Arsene Wenger's Arsenal. What followed was a scintillating tie which the Gunners edged 3-2, thanks to a late Theo Walcott goal.

Both performances provided a shot in the arm as the Seagulls embarked on the second half of their league campaign, with ex-England international Matthew Upson brought in to strengthen the defence, likewise Leo Ulloa to bolster the attack. The Argentine forward would prove to be the focal point of the team's attack on the Play-Off spots, netting the Amex's first hat-trick in a 4-1 win against Huddersfield Town, likewise a brace in the 3-0 home defeat of rivals Crystal Palace.

The campaign would also witness the stadium's highest win to date, a 6-1 hammering of Blackpool, while successive wins at Leeds United [2-1] and at home to Wolves [2-0] ensured the Seagulls went into the Play-Offs against Palace in a confident frame of mind.

A 0-0 draw at Selhurst Park in the first leg only accelerated the belief that the Seagulls were heading to Wembley, but Wilfried Zaha had other ideas as his two goals in the final 20 minutes gave the Eagles a 2-0 victory.

The new stadium had suffered its first major blow and it was a tough result to take given the opposition. Those feelings of disappointment were accelerated further given the squad that had been assembled that season. As it was, the defeat proved to be the end of an era, with manager Gus Poyet parting company with the club that summer, and Oscar Garcia brought into the hotseat.

2021/22
PRE-SEASON
PREPARATIONS

With the Seagulls' 2021/22 Premier League campaign kicking off away to Burnley on Saturday 14 August 2021, head coach Graham Potter, his staff and the players had the sole objective of making sure they were fully prepared for that first whistle of the new season.

The ongoing Covid-19 pandemic resulted in this pre-season being drastically different to a number of its predecessors. With overseas travel proving an ongoing challenge, there was no foreign training camp and just three first-team fixtures were officially scheduled ahead of the all-important trip to Lancashire.

After a number of tough training sessions, Albion returned to action on Saturday 24 July when they began their preparations for the new season with a goalless draw against Scottish champions Rangers at Ibrox.

It was a strong squad that arrived in Glasgow, despite the absence of 12 players including Albion's Euro 2020 and Copa America players, Alexis Mac Allister and Tudor Baluta, who were at the Tokyo Olympics, and Lewis Dunk, Danny Welbeck, Tariq Lamptey and Adam Webster.

Graham Potter fielded two separate teams with Kjell Scherpen and Enock Mwepu making their debuts in the first half while U23s' Marc Leonard, Ayo Tanimowo, Taylor Richards, James Furlong and Antef Tsoungui all got opportunities to impress after the break.

There was no surprise to hear Shane Duffy getting stick from the Ibrox faithful following his loan spell at Celtic last season, but the defender was in the right place at the right time early on to keep out Cedric Itten's shot after he had dispossessed Scherpen.

Albion gradually worked their way into the game and Dan Burn, under pressure from a couple of defenders, headed Pascal Gross' corner narrowly over, and just before the break, Andi Zeqiri tested the home 'keeper with a shot from distance.

Albion's 11 changes at the break resulted in the visitors enjoying a decent spell of possession at the start of the second half as the new-look team settled down, with Steven Alzate operating on the right of the back three and Solly March and Percy Tau in behind Florin Andone.

March, fit again after injury wrecked the second half of last season, made a couple of good bursts down the left, but it was Rangers who nearly opened the scoring in the 62nd minute when John Lundstram clipped a left-foot effort from outside the box against the bar.

There was a big cheer from the 8,000 crowd - the largest at Ibrox since March 2020 - when ex-Albion defender Connor Goldson came on for the last 20 minutes. With 22 Albion players tasting match action, this proved a useful workout despite the game ending goalless.

A week on from their Ibrox stalemate, Brighton enjoyed their first win of pre-season as they defeated Championship side Luton Town at Kenilworth Road on Saturday 31 July 2021.

There were just six minutes on the clock when the hosts had a glorious opportunity to take the lead as Elijah Adebayo managed to evade the challenge of Dan Burn down the right of the box. He pulled the ball back for Harry Cornick, who looked certain to fire his side into the lead, but he scuffed his effort from six yards out and Burn was able to clear.

Luton would rue not taking the opportunity as three minutes later Adam Lallana played Aaron Connolly in and the Republic of Ireland international slotted past Simon Sluga in confident fashion.

The Hatters could have levelled on the half-hour mark when Solly March's header back to Robert Sanchez lacked power. Cornick pounced on it, but his effort from an acute angle was a relatively easy one for Sanchez to deal with. March was quick to make amends down the other end when five minutes later his neat cut-back to the edge of the box was expertly tucked away by Enock Mwepu, finding the bottom-right corner.

Town did get back in the game just before the break when Cornick intercepted Burn's sliced pass and completed the straightforward job of rolling the ball into the net.

Any thoughts Luton had of sharing the spoils came to an end in the 63rd minute as Florin Andone found Percy Tau, who ran at goal, sitting Gabe Osho down, before expertly finding the bottom-left corner.

The Seagulls rounded off their pre-season programme with a 2-0 defeat to La Liga outfit Getafe at the Amex on Saturday 7 August. There were first pre-season run-outs for Adam Webster, Lewis Dunk and Leandro Trossard, as Potter used 21 players a week ahead of the big Premier League kick-off at Turf Moor.

The visitors took the lead in impressive fashion midway through the first half, when Erick Cabaco headed into the bottom right corner from 12 yards following a Getafe free-kick out wide. Pascal Gross came close to an instant reply for Albion, firing a free-kick from the edge of the box straight into David Soria's arms.

Getafe coach and former Spain international Michel would have been pleased with his side's performance and they nearly got a second when Damian Suarez's thunderbolt from 30 yards flew narrowly wide of the top-left corner three minutes before the half-time whistle.

The introduction of Trossard at the break nearly had an immediate impact as the Belgium international sat a Getafe defender down before picking out Joel Veltman on the other side of the box in the 52nd minute. The wing-back saw his cross blocked, but followed it up with a stinging effort that Soria did well to palm away, before he pulled off an instinctive diving save to keep out Aaron Connolly's flick.

It was very much against the run of play when Getafe scored again midway through the second half. Enes Unal's low effort was saved expertly by Robert Sanchez, but the keeper could do nothing about a free-kick in the visitors' favour moments later when David Timor found the bottom-right corner from 20 yards.

A disappointing result, but there were plenty of positives for Graham Potter's Seagulls, not least the noise and encouragement generated by a crowd of 7,091.

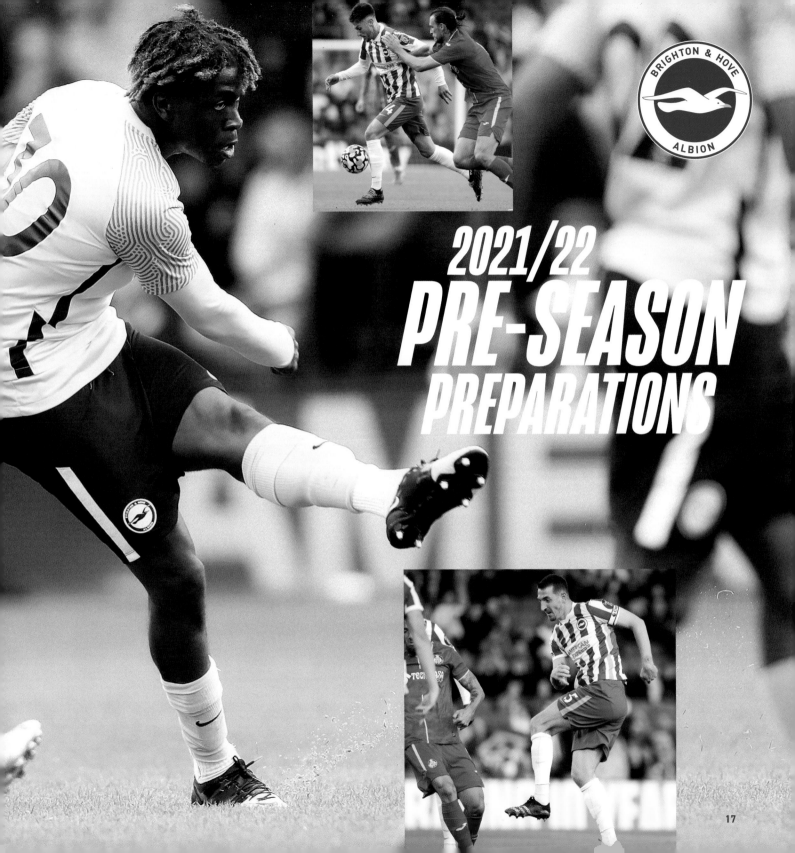

2021/22 PRE-SEASON PREPARATIONS

Such was the quality of goals they had to choose from, Albion fans were somewhat spoilt for choice when it came to casting their vote for the club's 2020/21 Goal of the Season award.

In a season when fans were in the main unable to attend matches at the Amex Stadium due to the ongoing coronavirus pandemic, Graham Potter's side managed to lift the spirits of the club's supporters with some scintillating football and stunning strikes.

After much deliberation, the supporters' votes confirmed that a sensational Amex Stadium strike from forward Danny Welbeck against Leeds United would win the former England striker the club's prestigious award.

Welbeck's goal was not just spectacular, but vitally important too as it secured the Seagulls a vital three points against the Yorkshire club in May 2021.

Already a goal to the good against a Leeds side that were looking to extend an impressive six-match unbeaten run, Welbeck secured the win with 11 minutes remaining. The former England forward produced a wonderful piece of individual skill with a Cruyff-like turn to escape the attentions of Leeds defender Pascal Struijk before firing a low angled drive past visiting 'keeper Illan Meslier.

This win gave Albion a Premier League double over the newly-promoted Elland Road outfit, but more importantly moved the club to within touching distance of securing top-flight football for a fifth consecutive season and with four fixtures still remaining.

The goal certainly capped off a memorable afternoon's work from Welbeck who had been upended for a 14th-minute penalty from which Pascal Gross had given Albion the lead.

The skill, technique and sharp finish were always going to see 30-year-old Welbeck's goal as a main contender for the Goal of the Season accolade. However, it still had some serious competition to edge past including the goals shown here, which also came into the reckoning at the end-of-season vote in June.

Winning the Goal of the Season award certainly capped off a memorable debut season at Brighton for Welbeck who joined the Seagulls in October 2020 as a free agent following his release from Watford.

After agreeing a one-year contract at the Amex, the former Manchester United, Arsenal and Watford man made his debut against Tottenham Hotspur on 1 November 2020. Just three games into his Brighton career and Welbeck had registered his first goal for his new club when his 12th-minute opener set the Seagulls on the road to victory at Aston Villa on 21 November.

Welbeck ended the campaign with six Premier League goals from 24 appearances and was rewarded with a new contract for the 2021/22 season at the Amex.

GOAL
OF THE
SEASON

Danny
WELBECK

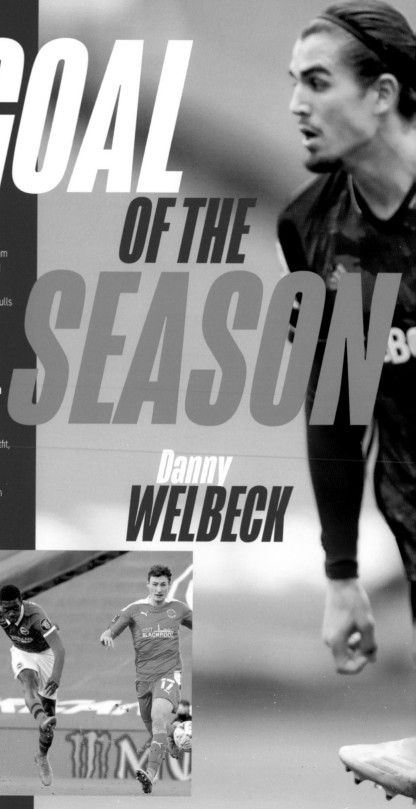

2nd

3rd

1st – *Danny* WELBECK
v Leeds United (H) · 1 May 2021

2nd – *Yves* BISSOUMA
v Blackpool (H FA CUP) · 23 January 2021

3rd – *Leandro* TROSSARD
v Man City (H) · 18 May 2021

4th – *Neal* MAUPAY
v Leeds United (A) · 16 January 2021

5th – *Yves* BISSOUMA
v Everton (A) · 3 October 2020

4th

5th

Oscar Garcia was a relative unknown when he walked through the doors at the Amex, but came with a proven CV, having been a Barcelona midfield graduate and later youth-team coach at the Catalan giants. He also ensured the Spanish-speaking influence and playing style at the club remained, and it was hoped that continuity would result in another promotion push.

He didn't get off to the best of starts, with a 2-1 opening-day defeat at Leeds United followed by a 2-1 home defeat against Derby County, but back-to-back victories at the end of August against Birmingham and Burnley [who would go on to secure automatic promotion] got the side – boosted by the permanent arrival of Matthew Upson from Stoke City, likewise left-back Stephen Ward on loan from Wolves – back on track.

Albion would lose just twice in their next 15 games, including consecutive wins against Doncaster, Blackburn and Wigan in November, which was rewarded with the Manager of the Month award for Garcia – and by the turn of the year, the Seagulls were sitting level on points with Ipswich Town in sixth place.

In typical Championship fashion, Albion then embarked on a rollercoaster ride of results, but consecutive 2-0 home defeats against Ipswich and Middlesbrough in March, likewise a defeat at Sheffield Wednesday, blew hopes of promotion off course. There was little expectation, therefore, as the Seagulls headed to champions-elect Leicester City in early April, but goals from Leo Ulloa (2), Ward and Jesse Lingard, who had arrived on loan from Manchester United, provided a much-needed boost.

Ahead of the final day of the season, Albion sat a point behind sixth-placed Reading; the Royals faced Burnley at home, while the Seagulls travelled to Nottingham Forest, along with a large and vociferous away following. Matt Derbyshire gave the Reds a first-half lead, only for Ward to equalise eight minutes after the re-start. With Reading losing 2-1, the City Ground was reminiscent of the Amex, given the noise created from the away end, but there were hushed tones just minutes later when news filtered through of an equaliser at the Madejski Stadium.

The remainder of the half was a tense, anxious affair. There was an air of resignation for some, but as the game ticked into the 92nd minute, sub Craig Mackail-Smith sent in a delightful cross from the left flank that was met by the head of Ulloa. The back of the net rippled, the fans behind the goal erupted, and Albion had booked their Play-Off place in the most dramatic of circumstances.

Sadly, history would repeat itself in the Play-Offs, with a frustrating 2-1 home defeat to Derby County in the first leg setting up a comfortable 6-2 win for the Rams over two legs. Dreams of the Premier League were scuppered once again, with Oscar handing in his resignation soon after.

LEO ULLOA CELEBRATES HIS LAST-MINUTE WINNER AT FOREST

10 YEARS AT THE AMEX

BRIGHTON & HOVE ALBION

2013/14

OSCAR GARCIA

HEAD COACH: *Oscar Garcia*
LEAGUE: *Championship*
FINAL LEAGUE POSITION: *6th*
TOP SCORER: *Leonardo Ulloa* (16 IN ALL COMPETITION
LEAGUE WINS: *19*
LEAGUE GOALS SCORED: *55*
LEAGUE POINTS WON: *72*
AVERAGE HOME ATTENDANCE: *27,283*
PLAYER OF THE SEASON: *Matthew Upson*

ADRIAN COLUNGA CELEBRATES SCORING
THE FIRST GOAL AT CRAVEN COTTAGE

MANAGER: *Sami Hyypia/Chris Hughton*

LEAGUE: *Championship*

FINAL LEAGUE POSITION: *20th*

TOP SCORER: *Lewis Dunk & João Teixeira*
(6 EACH IN ALL COMPETITIONS)

LEAGUE WINS: *10*

LEAGUE GOALS SCORED: *44*

LEAGUE POINTS WON: *47*

AVERAGE HOME ATTENDANCE: *25,660*

PLAYER OF THE SEASON: *Inigo Calderon*

2014/15

CHRIS HUGHTON
KICKS OFF AT BRENTFORD

For Albion fans, the opening seasons at the Amex had, Play-Offs aside, been an enjoyable experience, but season 2014/15 proved an extremely difficult watch. With former Liverpool captain Sami Hyypia appointed as successor to Oscar Garcia, having guided Bayer Leverkusen to fourth place in the Bundesliga the previous season, optimism remained high.

There was a changing of the guard within the squad, with the likes of Andrea Orlandi, David Lopez and Leo Ulloa all leaving the club, while home-based arrivals included goalkeeper David Stockdale, defender Aaron Hughes and striker Sam Baldock. Loan arrivals also included Joao Teixeira from Liverpool and Aston Villa duo Joe Bennett and Gary Gardner.

The changes made for an extended transition, and an opening day 1-0 home defeat against Sheffield Wednesday set the tone for what would follow. Just two Championship wins from 15 games – back-to-back victories against Leeds United and Bolton in late August – left the side sitting uncomfortably in 21st place. Former Albion favourite Elliott Bennett and ex-England international Darren Bent arrived on loan to add some much-needed impetus to the side's attack in November, but the Seagulls picked up just one more win prior to the festive period, resulting in Hyypia's departure.

Assistant manager Nathan Jones stepped in to take the reins on a temporary basis and his promotion had the desired effect as a last-minute equaliser from Inigo Calderon secured a 2-2 draw with Reading at the Amex on Boxing Day. Three days later he impressed further by guiding the side to a 2-0 win at Fulham, paving the way the appointment of Chris Hughton on New Year's Eve as the club's fourth boss of the Amex era.

The former Tottenham defender came with an excellent CV, having guided Newcastle United to promotion from the Championship, and he made the perfect start with a 2-0 FA Cup win at Brentford and 1-0 Championship victory at Charlton Athletic.

The Cup run came to an end in the fourth round, with another thrilling 3-2 reverse against eventual winners Arsenal, but all focus was now on the Championship and ensuring the club retained its second-tier status.

While there would be bumps in the road, including a seven-game winless game at the end of the season, victories against Ipswich, Birmingham, Leeds, Derby and Blackburn - with four of the wins coming at the Amex - helped successfully steer the side away from the bottom three. Albion ended the campaign in 20th place, some six points clear of the drop zone, with anticipation that the following campaign would be much improved with Hughton's feet now firmly under the table.

BRUNO

AMEX HERO

BRUNO CELEBRATES HIS FIRST ALBION GOAL V BOLTON, 2012

When Brighton & Hove Albion acquired the services of 31-year-old right-back Bruno as a free agent in June 2012, few would have anticipated the level of success and popularity that the Spaniard would enjoy at the Amex.

Ahead of what was only the club's second season at the new stadium, Bruno agreed a two-year deal with the Seagulls following three seasons with Valencia. Having begun his career with Espanyol, he also plied his trade in his homeland with Lleida and Almeria before moving to the Mestalla in 2009.

After being handed an Albion debut in a League Cup tie away to Swindon Town, Bruno went on to become a regular face at right-back in 2012/13. He made 30 Championship appearances and scored his first goal for the club in a 1-1 draw with Bolton Wanderers at the Amex in November 2012 as Gus Poyet's side reached the end-of-season Play-Offs.

Over the following four seasons, Bruno really made the right-back shirt his own with a plethora of outstanding defensive displays which won him the respect of teammates, coaches and supporters alike.

A star performer once again in 2013/14 as Albion again qualified for the Play-Offs, he also played an important role as the club battled successfully against relegation following the appointment of Chris Hughton in 2014/15. Even at the age of 35, the classy Spaniard was ever-present in the Seagulls' 2015/16 promotion near-miss and his performances won him a place in the PFA's Championship Team of the Season.

Bruno and his teammates put the agony of missing out in 2015/16 firmly behind them as the club ended a 34-year wait for promotion back to the top flight in 2016/17. Brighton ended a sensational season as Championship runners-up and sealed promotion to the Premier League with captain Bruno missing just four of the Seagulls' 46-game league schedule. For a second consecutive campaign, he was again named in the PFA's Championship Team of the Season.

Although some felt his age may prevent him from performing at Premier League level, Bruno continued to confound the critics. He made his Premier League debut on the opening day of the 2017/18 season at home to title favourites Manchester City. A further 24 Premier League appearances followed when his calm defending went an awful long way to helping the club survive their first season back in the top flight.

Despite suffering a hamstring injury during the opening match of 2018/19, and losing his place to fellow Spaniard Martin Montoya, his return to the team coincided with three consecutive winning clean sheets in October 2018. He also played in the early rounds of the Seagulls' 2019 FA Cup campaign and played his part in helping set the team on their way to the semi-final stage. With Premier League safety secured, Bruno announced his retirement in May 2019 and played his final game for the club against Premier League champions Manchester City at the Amex.

On what was an emotional afternoon at the Amex, Bruno enhanced his legendary reputation with the Albion fans by ending his post-match speech of appreciation and farewell with the words:

"Once a Seagull, always a Seagull."

BRUNO BIDS AN EMOTIONAL FAREWELL
TO HIS PLAYING DAYS AT THE AMEX

FULL NAME:	Bruno Saltor Grau
DATE OF BIRTH:	1 October 1980
PLACE OF BIRTH:	El Masnou, Spain
POSITION:	Defender

SEAGULLS APPEARANCES	SEAGULLS GOALS
235	**6**

LEAGUE:	225	LEAGUE:	6
FA CUP:	6	FA CUP:	0
LEAGUE CUP:	2	LEAGUE CUP:	0
OTHER:	2	OTHER:	0

ALBION DEBUT:	Swindon Town 3-0 Brighton & Hove Albion 14 August 2012 · League Cup
ALBION HONOURS:	Championship runner-up 2016/17

A youth-team player with Levante in his homeland, Rob moved to the Albion in June 2015. To gain first-team experience, he joined Forest Green Rovers on loan in 2018/19, making his debut in a 4-1 win at Grimsby Town.

He made 17 League Two appearances before stepping up a division to join Rochdale the following season. The highlight of his time at Spotland was a Carabao Cup tie at Manchester United, where he gained plenty of plaudits with the game going to penalties.

He returned to Sussex ahead of the 2020/21 season and following a pre-season injury sustained to Christian Walton, was promoted to the first-team squad. On 1 November he made his debut for the club, in a 2-1 defeat against Tottenham, and was soon elevated to top spot.

He soon established himself as the Seagulls' first-choice 'keeper – with Mat Ryan joining Arsenal on loan as a result – and penned a new contract in February 2021. His excellent form was rewarded with a call-up to the Spain squad for Euro 2020 and the World Cup qualifiers, making his debut against Georgia in September.

Tariq came through the ranks at Chelsea, joining the club's academy at the age of eight. He went on to make his Premier League debut, as a substitute, against Arsenal at the Emirates Stadium in December 2019 and played a key role as the Blues came from behind to win 2-1.

He joined the Albion the following month, but had to bide his time to break into the first team. It duly arrived at Leicester City that June, where his marauding runs helped the Seagulls to a solid 0-0 draw.

Be it in the full-back or wing-back position, his pace has been a real asset for Graham Potter's side when either attacking or defending. His form earned a call-up to the England U21 international set-up and he made his debut against Austria in September 2020. Sadly, injury curtailed his progress in the second half of last season but he is now back and looking to continue his excellent progress in 2021/22.

Robert SANCHEZ

*POSITION: **Goalkeeper** DoB: **18 November 1997** BIRTHPLACE: **Cartagena, Spain***

02

Tariq **LAMPTEY**

POSITION: *Defender* DOB: *30 September 2000* BIRTHPLACE: *London*

PREMIER LEAGUE SQUAD 21/22

25

03

Marc CUCURELLA

POSITION: *Defender* **DoB:** *22 July 1998* **BIRTHPLACE:** *Alella, Spain*

Marc came through the system with Barcelona and emerged as a regular in the club's B team. He made his senior debut in a Copa del Rey game against Real Murcia in October 2017, coming on as a late substitute for Lucas Digne, which proved to be his only appearance for the club.

In August 2018, he was loaned to fellow La Liga side Eibar, where he went on to establish himself as a regular in his one season at the club. He was then loaned out to Getafe in July 2019 and another full season of top-flight football clinched a permanent move to the 'Azulones'.

With a flourishing reputation, either as a wide player or full-back, Marc was called up to the Spain national squad in the summer of 2021 and made his debut against Lithuania in a friendly in June. On 31 August, he joined the Seagulls on a five-year contract and made his debut in the 1-0 win at Brentford.

PREMIER LEAGUE SQUAD 21/22

Adam WEBSTER

POSITION: *Defender* **DoB:** *4 January 1995* **BIRTHPLACE:** *Chichester*

A player who featured in all three EFL divisions with his first club Portsmouth, Adam made his debut against West Ham United in the Championship, aged 17, in January 2012.

He went on to appear 81 times for the club before a move to Ipswich Town in June 2016. He spent two seasons in the second tier with the Blues, then switched to Bristol City, where he was crowned Player of the Year in his one season at the club.

The centre-back joined Albion from the Robins in August 2019 and soon became one of the first names on Graham Potter's team sheet. He made his Premier League debut that same month at Manchester City and also gained praise from Pep Guardiola for his performance at the Etihad Stadium last season.

He also netted the equaliser in the memorable 3-2 victory against the champions at the Amex in May. Adam is a former England U19 international with six caps to his name.

While the club captain is Brighton born and bred, Lewis actually started his football career with Wimbledon, but left when the Dons relocated to Milton Keynes.

He joined Albion's centre of excellence at U12 level and progressed through the ranks to make his senior debut in a League One encounter at MK Dons in May 2010. He made a further five league appearances the following season, as the Seagulls won the title, before emerging as a first-team regular in the club's debut campaign at the Amex Stadium.

A commanding presence at centre-half, 'Dunky' has gone on to make over 300 league appearances for the Seagulls and his form in the Premier League was rewarded with an England debut against the United States in November 2018. There were calls for a return to the Three Lions' set-up in 2020/21 where his imperious displays for the Seagulls were rewarded with his fourth Players' Player of the Season award.

Lewis DUNK 05

POSITION: *Defender* DoB: *21 November 1991* BIRTHPLACE: *Brighton*

27

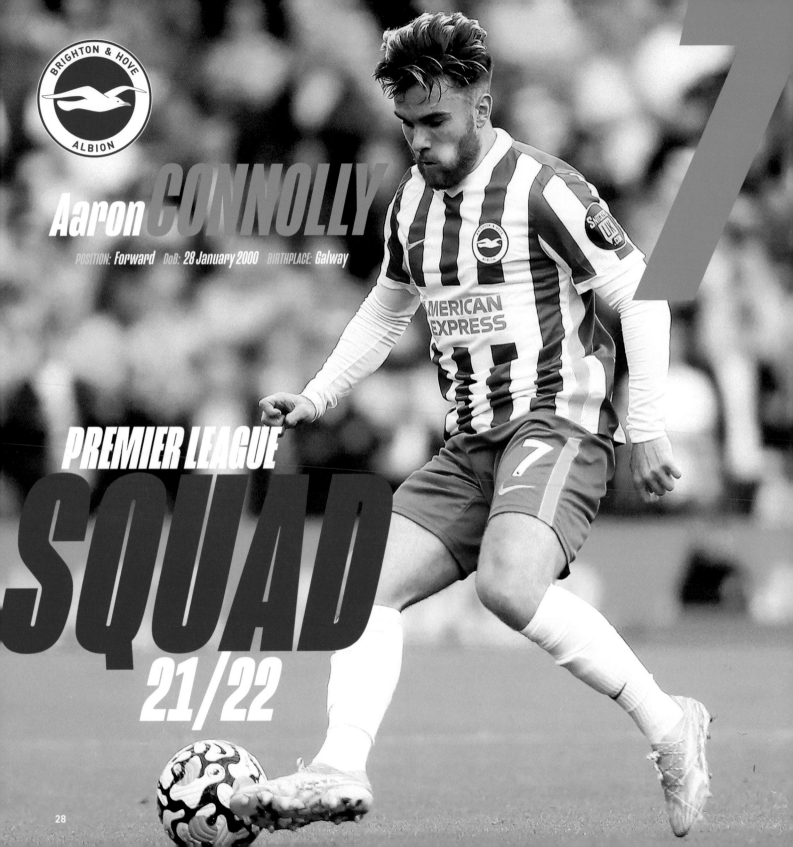

Aaron **CONNOLLY**

POSITION: **Forward**   DoB: **28 January 2000**   BIRTHPLACE: **Galway**

PREMIER LEAGUE
SQUAD
21/22

28

Aaron was a junior player with Mervue United, in Galway, where his goalscoring form earned a trial with the Seagulls in 2016. He impressed to earn a two-year scholarship with the Albion U18 side, but was soon fast-tracked to the U23 set-up.

His first-team debut arrived in the EFL Cup against Barnet in January 2017, prior to a spell on loan at Luton Town in the second half of the 2018/19 season. His breakthrough campaign with the Albion came following Graham Potter's arrival at the Amex and he scored his first senior goal in August 2019, in an EFL Cup tie at Bristol Rovers.

Connolly created national headlines after netting a memorable brace in a 3-0 Premier League win against Tottenham Hotspur that October at the Amex, and he went on to make his Republic of Ireland debut a few days later, as a late substitute in a 0-0 Euro 2020 qualifier against Georgia in Tblisi.

Born in the Ivory Coast, but raised in Mali, 'Biss' started his career at the Majestic SC academy in 2009 before making his breakthrough with Malian Premiere Division club AS Real Bamako in 2014.

He spent two seasons with the club before a move to French club Lille in July 2018, where he played under current Leeds boss Marcelo Bielsa. The central midfielder made 47 Ligue 1 appearances in two seasons before a move to the Seagulls in July 2018.

He made his Albion debut the following month in a 2-0 Premier League defeat at Watford and while he has always been in and around the first-team set-up, the Mali international really came to the fore following Dale Stephens' departure in the summer of 2020.

Indeed, Bissouma caught the eye with a number of impressive performances at the heart of the side, and he has now made over 100 appearances for the Seagulls.

Yves BISSOUMA

POSITION: *Midfielder* DoB: *30 August 1996* BIRTHPLACE: *Issia, Ivory Coast*

Making his Ligue 1 debut for Nice at the age of just 16 years and 32 days, Maupay was an injury-time substitute in a 3-2 win against Brest. He was a first-team squad regular for three seasons and also spent time at Saint-Etienne before a move to Brentford in July 2017.

In his first season at Griffin Park, Neal scored 12 Championship goals, but went on to net 25 league goals in 43 appearances in 2018/19 to win the club's Player of the Season award. He moved to the Albion that August and scored on his Premier League debut at Watford later in the month.

The former France U21 international, with two caps and one goal to his name, has gone on to become the Seagulls' leading scorer in the top flight for the past two seasons and has earned plenty of plaudits for his tireless running in the forward positions.

Alexis comes from a footballing family, with his father Carlos a former left-back for Boca Juniors and the Argentina national team, while his older brothers Francis and Kevin are also professionals.

He started out in the Argentinos Juniors' youth set-up and went on to make his senior debut in October 2016 against Central Cordoba. He appeared 33 times in the Primera Division, scoring five times, before joining the Albion in January 2019.

As part of the deal, he was immediately loaned back to Argentinos Juniors, before joining his brother Kevin at Boca Juniors that summer. He appeared in ten league games for the Argentine giants, scoring twice, before a return to England.

A Premier League debut came shortly before the Covid-19 pandemic hit the country, against Wolves in March 2020, but Alexis' breakthrough campaign came in 2020/21, where he appeared 21 times in the top flight and netted a memorable 90th-minute equaliser at rivals Crystal Palace.

Neal MAUPAY

9

POSITION: *Forward*   DoB: *14 August 1996*   BIRTHPLACE: *Versailles, France*

10

PREMIER LEAGUE
SQUAD
21/22

Alexis **MAC ALLISTER**

POSITION: Midfielder   DoB: 24 December 1998   BIRTHPLACE: Santa Rosa, Argentina

31

Leandro TROSSARD

POSITION: *Midfielder* DoB: *4 December 1994* BIRTHPLACE: *Maasmechelen, Belgium*

PREMIER LEAGUE SQUAD 21/22

11

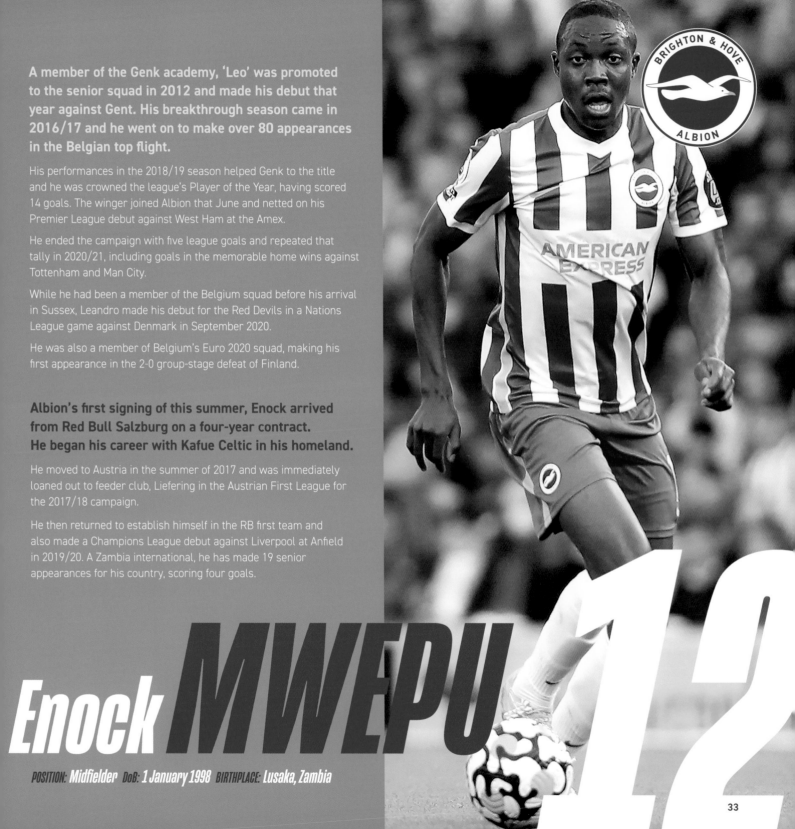

A member of the Genk academy, 'Leo' was promoted to the senior squad in 2012 and made his debut that year against Gent. His breakthrough season came in 2016/17 and he went on to make over 80 appearances in the Belgian top flight.

His performances in the 2018/19 season helped Genk to the title and he was crowned the league's Player of the Year, having scored 14 goals. The winger joined Albion that June and netted on his Premier League debut against West Ham at the Amex.

He ended the campaign with five league goals and repeated that tally in 2020/21, including goals in the memorable home wins against Tottenham and Man City.

While he had been a member of the Belgium squad before his arrival in Sussex, Leandro made his debut for the Red Devils in a Nations League game against Denmark in September 2020.

He was also a member of Belgium's Euro 2020 squad, making his first appearance in the 2-0 group-stage defeat of Finland.

Albion's first signing of this summer, Enock arrived from Red Bull Salzburg on a four-year contract. He began his career with Kafue Celtic in his homeland.

He moved to Austria in the summer of 2017 and was immediately loaned out to feeder club, Liefering in the Austrian First League for the 2017/18 campaign.

He then returned to establish himself in the RB first team and also made a Champions League debut against Liverpool at Anfield in 2019/20. A Zambia international, he has made 19 senior appearances for his country, scoring four goals.

Enock MWEPU 12

POSITION: *Midfielder* DoB: *1 January 1998* BIRTHPLACE: *Lusaka, Zambia*

Following in the footsteps of his father Stephan, who played professional football for Karlsruher, Pascal made his Bundesliga debut for Hoffenheim, in a 4-0 defeat to Wolfsburg in May 2009.

Having made five top-flight appearances, he moved to his father's former club, where he emerged as a regular in Bundesliga 2 in the 2011/12 season. That summer he was on the move again, to fellow second-tier club FC Ingolstadt, playing a key role in their promotion in 2014/15.

He remained a regular for the following two seasons before joining the Seagulls ahead of the club's debut Premier League campaign. He made history by scoring Albion's first-ever top-flight goal, in a 3-1 win against West Bromwich Albion that September.

Pascal went on to make his 100th appearance in an EFL Cup tie at Preston in September 2020, where he was made captain. Later in the season he also skippered the side to a memorable 3-2 home win against champions Manchester City.

A member of the AFC Bournemouth centre of excellence, Adam joined Southampton's academy as a 12-year-old in 2000. He went on to make his debut in a League Cup win against Yeovil Town in August 2006 before establishing himself in the first team in 2008/09.

The central midfielder went on to become a key player as the club won successive promotions to reach the Premier League in 2012, and his form in two top-flight seasons clinched a move to Liverpool. While at Anfield, he was a member of the squad that won the Champions League in 2019 and picked up a Premier League winners' medal the following season.

Heading back south with the Seagulls in the summer of 2020, he came off the bench to help the side to a famous 1-0 win at Anfield in February 2021. While he made only 16 Premier League starts, he appeared 30 times in the top flight last season. Having won 34 England caps, Lallana was named the Three Lions' Player of the Year in 2016.

Pascal GROSS

POSITION: **Midfielder**   *DoB:* **15 June 1991**   *BIRTHPLACE:* **Mannhein, Germany**

14

Adam **LALLANA**

POSITION: *Midfielder*   DoB: *10 May 1988*   BIRTHPLACE: *St Albans*

PREMIER LEAGUE
SQUAD
21/22

35

In 2014, Jakub joined Lech Poznan's academy and by April 2018 he had made his first-team debut in a 3-1 win at Wisla Krakow.

His breakthrough campaign in the Polish top flight came in 2019/20, where he made 26 appearances, scoring five goals as the side finished runners-up and qualified for the Europa League.

In October 2020, he joined the Albion, but was immediately loaned back to his former club. He returned to Sussex following the club's exit from the Europa League and went on to make his Albion debut in an FA Cup tie at Leicester in February 2021.

He has since remained part of the squad and has also established himself in the Poland set-up, having made his debut in a Nations League defeat against the Netherlands in September 2020. He scored his second goal for his country in a 2-1 defeat to England in March 2021.

A summer arrival from Ajax, Kjell started his career with hometown club Emmen, where he progressed to become a regular in the Eredivisie in 2018/19.

He joined Ajax that summer and following a prolonged spell with Jong Ajax, he made his senior debut in April 2021 following an injury to first-choice 'keeper Maarten Stekelenburg.

The former Netherlands U19 international made two top-flight appearances and also appeared in the Europa League against Roma before his switch to the Amex Stadium.

15 Jakub MODER

POSITION: *Midfielder* DoB: *7 April 1999* BIRTHPLACE: *Szczecinek, Poland*

PREMIER LEAGUE SQUAD 21/22

Kjell SCHERPEN

POSITION: *Goalkeeper* DoB: *23 January 2000* BIRTHPLACE: *Emmen, Netherlands*

Steven ALZATE

POSITION: **Midfielder** DoB: **8 September 1998** BIRTHPLACE: **Camden**

The Londoner started his career at Leyton Orient, making his debut in a 4-1 defeat at Stevenage in February 2017. He scored his first goal in the very next game, a 4-0 victory against Newport County, and went on to make 12 appearances for the O's.

In July 2017 he joined the Albion, linking up with the club's U23 squad, and had to wait two years to make his first-team debut, via a loan spell at Swindon, playing the full match in an EFL Cup win against Bristol Rovers. The versatile midfielder made his Premier League debut at Newcastle United that September, earning the Man of the Match award in a 0-0 draw, and his Amex debut came a few weeks later, against Tottenham, where he started in a 3-0 victory.

Born to Colombian parents, Steven made his international debut in November 2019 against Peru, and his first start came the following week against Ecuador.

18

PREMIER LEAGUE
SQUAD
21/22

Danny WELBECK

POSITION: Forward   DoB: 26 November 1990   BIRTHPLACE: Manchester

Danny made his way through the Manchester United youth set-up to make his debut in a League Cup win against Middlesbrough in September 2008.

During his time at Old Trafford, he won the Premier League in 2012/13 and two League Cup winners' medals in 2009 and 2010. With 20 goals from 92 top-flight appearances, he joined Arsenal in September 2014 and went on to net 22 times in 88 Premier League games. Sadly, his time at the Emirates was beset by injury problems, but he picked up an FA Cup winners' medal before joining Watford ahead of the 2019/20 season.

His one season at Vicarage Road would end in relegation, but he remained at the highest level, having joined the Albion in October 2020 on a one-year contract. Danny, with 42 England caps and 16 goals to his name, emerged as an important figure both on and off the pitch and netted the club's Goal of the Season, with a sublime turn and shot against Leeds United. His performances were rewarded with a new one-year contract in June 2021.

Solly had spells at Crystal Palace and Eastbourne Borough before making his competitive debut playing for Isthmian Premier League club Lewes, in September 2011, against Aveley.

Soon after, he joined the Albion, despite interest from Millwall and Newcastle, and linked up with the development squad. He was voted the club's Young Player of the Season in 2013 and went on to make his debut that August in a 2-1 Championship defeat against Derby.

March has made over 200 appearances for the Seagulls – and netted one of the goals which secured promotion to the Premier League, against Wigan in April 2017 – but 2020/21 was, arguably, his best to date in a blue and white shirt.

Employed by Graham Potter as a left wing-back, he showed great form and consistency until sustaining a knee injury in the memorable win at Liverpool which curtailed his season. Named by Gareth Southgate in the England U21 squad in May 2014, March went on to make three appearances, scoring once against Denmark.

Solly MARCH

POSITION: *Midfielder* **DoB:** *20 July 1994* **BIRTHPLACE:** *Eastbourne*

A product of Middlesbrough's academy, Jason made his professional bow on loan at League Two Northampton Town, in February 2010, against Cheltenham Town.

His Boro debut came that October against Chesterfield in the League Cup and he went on to make over 130 Championship appearances for the club. In September 2014 he joined Blackburn on a season-long loan deal, which was made permanent just three months later.

After three full seasons at Ewood Park, he returned to the north east, joining newly-relegated Championship side Sunderland, but featured just 18 times as the Black Cats were again relegated. In June 2018 he headed south to Brighton and while he had not made a Premier League appearance in his first three seasons, he made five appearances in cup competitions, including four in 2020/21.

He also emerged as the preferred back-up to first-choice keeper Robert Sanchez last season, earning a new contract with the club.

Shane, a former Everton youngster, made his professional debut for the Toffees against AEK Athens in the Europa League in December 2009.

Loan spells at Burnley, Scunthorpe and Yeovil followed before a move to Blackburn in 2014. He spent a little over two years with the Ewood Park club then made a switch to the Albion in August 2016.

He went on to play a key role in the Seagulls' promotion to the Premier League and was voted the club's Player of the Season in the top flight in 2018/19. The Republic of Ireland international spent last season on loan at Celtic, but has returned to re-establish himself as a key player in Graham Potter's defence.

23 Jason STEELE

POSITION: *Goalkeeper*   DoB: *18 August 1990*   BIRTHPLACE: *Newton Aycliffe*

40

24

PREMIER LEAGUE SQUAD 21/22

Shane **DUFFY**

POSITION: *Defender*   DoB: *1 January 1992*   BIRTHPLACE: *Derry*

27

PREMIER LEAGUE
SQUAD
21/22

Jurgen LOCADIA

POSITION: *Forward*
DoB: *7 November 1993*
BIRTHPLACE: *Emmen, Netherlands*

Haydon ROBERTS

POSITION: *Defender*   DoB: *10 May 2002*   BIRTHPLACE: *Brighton*

28

Starting his career with PSV Eindhoven, Jurgen made his senior debut in September 2011 against VVSB in a domestic cup match.

Having netted 45 Eredivisie goals in 127 appearances, he joined the Albion in January 2018 but found chances hard to come by. He has spent time on loan at Hoffenheim and FC Cincinnati before a return to Sussex this summer.

Homegrown centre-back Haydon came through the club's academy to make his senior debut at home to Aston Villa in the EFL Cup in September 2019.

He caught the eye with a fine performance, capped by a goal in the 3-1 defeat. His second appearance for the club came the following season against Portsmouth in the same competition - and within weeks he had penned a season-long loan move to League One Rochdale.

An England U18 international, he made 25 appearances for Dale before his return to Sussex. This season, Roberts has been elevated to the Albion first-team squad, making his first appearance of the campaign against Cardiff City in the EFL Cup.

Taylor joined Albion in July 2019 from Manchester City, before signing a new three-year contract with the club in August 2021.

The midfielder moved from Fulham to Manchester at the age of 14, breaking into City's U23s during the 2018/19 Premier League 2 campaign, making 15 league appearances, as well as five in the UEFA Youth League and four in the EFL Trophy. Richards ended the season with an impressive ten goals from 29 appearances, and continued his goalscoring form by hitting the winning penalty on his first pre-season appearance for Albion against Crawley Town.

The 20-year-old spent the 2020/21 season on loan with Doncaster Rovers, where he was a regular, scoring 11 goals in 48 outings. He went on to make his Premier League debut for Albion at the beginning of the 2021/22 campaign, in a 2-0 home defeat to Everton.

Taylor RICHARDS

POSITION: *Midfielder*   **DoB:** *4 December 2000*   **BIRTHPLACE:** *London*

Dan BURN

POSITION: *Defender*   DoB: *9 May 1992*   BIRTHPLACE: *Blyth*

PREMIER LEAGUE SQUAD 21/22

33

44

Released by boyhood heroes Newcastle United as a youngster, Dan played non-league football for Blyth Spartans, where he was spotted by then-League Two club Darlington.

He made his debut in December 2009 at Torquay United and with the club's financial issues, he played four times that season. Relegation to the Conference followed, but he was a shining light in 2010/11, courting attention from the Toon and Premier League Fulham.

He opted to head south, spending time on loan with Yeovil and Birmingham, but went on to make over 60 league appearances for the Cottagers. Two seasons then followed at Wigan Athletic, where he helped the Latics make an immediate return to the Championship in 2017/18, before joining the Seagulls that summer. He has since made over 60 Premier League appearances and in May 2021, scored his first goal for the club in the 3-2 home win over Manchester City.

A product of the Ajax academy, Joel went on to make his debut against NEC in August 2012. The following eight years saw him win three Eredivisie titles, the KNVB Cup, appear in a Champions League semi-final against Tottenham Hotspur, and pick up a Europa League runners-up medal against Manchester United.

A versatile player, who can also operate in midfield, he moved to Sussex in July 2020 and made his debut that September against Portsmouth in the Carabao Cup. While his appearances were more fleeting in the first half of the season, he established himself in the right wing-back position in 2021 following the long-term injury sustained by Tariq Lamptey.

His form for the Seagulls cemented his place in the Netherlands' Euro 2020 squad, having made his debut for his country in November 2013 against Colombia. He was also a member of the Netherlands' 2014 World Cup finals squad.

Joel VELTMAN 34

POSITION: *Defender* DoB: *15 January 1992* BIRTHPLACE: *IJmuiden, Netherlands*

With the previous season being a damage-limitation exercise, Chris Hughton had the summer to bring in his own players to the squad, with Tomer Hemed, Liam Rosenior, Gaetan Bong, Connor Goldson, Uwe Huenemeier and Jamie Murphy making their mark as the campaign got underway.

While all were welcome additions, none attracted the fanfare that accompanied the return of prodigal son, Bobby Zamora, after a 12-year absence from the club and just four days before the season opener against Nottingham Forest. It ensured a real buzz inside the Amex Stadium for the televised Friday night encounter against the Reds, fuelled further by Kazenga LuaLua's solitary goal which secured the Albion's first opening-day win since 2011/12.

With a solid defence, structured midfield and a real goal threat, the opening half of the campaign was hugely encouraging, with the side unbeaten in the Championship until mid-December. Eleven league wins were picked up along the way, with the run brought to an end by a 3-0 defeat at home to Middlesbrough before Christmas – a side that also had its sights set on promotion.

The Boro defeat was the start of a Yuletide wobble that brought a 0-0 draw at Brentford before successive defeats against Ipswich, Wolves and Rotherham. The arrival of Anthony Knockaert from Standard Liege and another former favourite in Steve Sidwell (on loan from Stoke) provided the perfect tonic as four successive wins against Blackburn, Huddersfield, Brentford and Bolton got the side back on track.

It was the start of a run which saw the Seagulls lose just once more all season, with springtime yielding a run of seven wins from eight games. The winter dip would ultimately prove costly as Burnley ran out title winners, and with Albion drawing their penultimate game of the season at home to Derby, they travelled to Middlesbrough on the final day. Victory would see the Albion promoted back to the top flight for the first time in 33 years but a 1-1 draw, not helped by a controversial red card handed to Dale Stephens shortly after he had equalised in the 55th minute, ensured the Teessiders were automatically promoted instead.

With injuries and suspensions mounting, the side had to pick themselves up for a Play-Off semi-final against Sheffield Wednesday, with the first leg at Hillsborough less than a week away. Missing the influential Lewis Dunk and Stephens, Albion also had Sidwell, Goldson and Hemed limp off injured during the game, while Anthony Knockaert was stretchered off after all three subs had been used. As a result, the Seagulls played the final 30 minutes with ten men and crashed to a 2-0 defeat.

It was a deficit the side couldn't claw back in the second leg, which finished 1-1, but for those present in the Amex that night, they witnessed a raucous first-half atmosphere that had yet to be beaten at the stadium.

ANTHONY KNOCKAERT CELEBRATES HIS STRIKE V BURNLEY, APRIL 2016

BRIGHTON & HOVE ALBION

YEARS AT THE AMEX

2015/16

BOBBY ZAMORA

MANAGER: *Chris Hughton*

LEAGUE: *Championship*

FINAL LEAGUE POSITION: *3rd*

TOP SCORER: *Tomer Hemed (17 IN ALL COMPETITIONS)*

LEAGUE WINS: *24*

LEAGUE GOALS SCORED: *72*

LEAGUE POINTS WON: *89*

AVERAGE HOME ATTENDANCE: *25,583*

PLAYER OF THE SEASON: *Beram Kayal*

MANAGER: *Chris Hughton*

LEAGUE: *Championship*

FINAL LEAGUE POSITION: *2nd*

TOP SCORER: *Glenn Murray*
(23 IN ALL COMPETITIONS)

LEAGUE WINS: *28*

LEAGUE GOALS SCORED: *74*

LEAGUE POINTS WON: *93*

AVERAGE HOME ATTENDANCE: *27,995*

PLAYER OF THE SEASON: *Anthony Knockaert*

2016/17

STOCKDALE'S PENALTY SAVE V SHEFFIELD WEDNESDAY

Given the double heartbreak that came at the end of the previous season, lesser teams could have struggled to come back from such a blow, but this Albion squad was made of sterner stuff.

From the very first meeting of pre-season, there was a steely determination to win promotion, using the bitter disappointment of the previous campaign as motivation.

While the squad was proven in the Championship, Chris Hughton made two pivotal signings: Shane Duffy arrived from Blackburn Rovers, to form an imperious partnership with Lewis Dunk in defence, while ex-Seagulls striker Glenn Murray was signed from Bournemouth, initially on loan, following a five-year absence.

Yet talk of a Play-Off hangover was rife in the opening weeks, with the side sitting 13th in the table in early September, following a 2-0 defeat at home to Brentford. It proved to be a pivotal moment, however, as the side embarked on an 18-game unbeaten run that stretched well into January, and included a 5-0 win against promotion favourites Norwich City at the Amex in late October.

With Murray bagging a hat-trick that afternoon, it laid down a marker to the rest of the division, while the striker was proving key to the promotion push – his last-gasp winner in a 2-1 win at Birmingham before Christmas a stand-out moment from the 23 league goals he would net come the end of the season.

During the winter months, the Amex witnessed six successive league wins, including victories against Fulham, Leeds United and the previous season's nemesis Sheffield Wednesday – a thrilling game that witnessed three red cards and a superb penalty double-save from David Stockdale. Another impressive sequence – six wins from seven league games – left Albion heading into the home game with Wigan Athletic on 17th April knowing victory would secure a place in the Premier League.

There was a real feeling of anticipation around the stadium, but any pre-match nerves were settled by goals in either half from Murray and Solly March. While Nick Powell netted late on to make for an uncomfortable finish, the scenes that greeted the final whistle will live long in the memory. The pitch quickly became a sea of celebrating fans; players were left in various states of undress and chairman Tony Bloom twirled his scarf in total joy from the directors' box.

Albion had finally reached the Promised Land and the challenge now was to win the title ahead of Newcastle United.

There would, however, be a hangover of different sorts as the side suffered back-to-back defeats to Norwich City and Bristol City. Victory at Aston Villa on the final day would still seal the deal, but an 89th minute Jack Grealish goal made it 1-1 on the day to leave Albion in second place. Once the disappointment wore off though, the smiles soon returned as the side looked forward to taking on the big guns come August…

LEWIS DUNK

AMEX HERO

BRIGHTON & HOVE ALBION

DUNK IN DEBUT ACTION V MK DONS, 2010

Born in Brighton, central-defender Lewis Dunk has emerged as the homegrown hero who has been at the heart of the club's successful era at the Amex Stadium.

Dunk first joined the club's centre of excellence as an U12 and worked his way through the age groups to land a scholarship with the U18 team.

After a number of highly-impressive performances as youth-team captain, Dunk was handed his first-team debut in the penultimate game of the Seagulls' 2009/10 League One campaign away to MK Dons. With Dunk featuring in the defence, it should be of little surprise that Brighton returned home with a clean sheet.

The following season he featured in eight first-team fixtures as the Seagulls won the League One title and subsequently began life at the Amex Stadium at Championship level.

With Adam El-Abd out with a long-term injury, Dunk made a first-team berth his own in 2011/12. He played in the very first league game at the Amex against Doncaster Rovers on opening day, and his form that season prompted a call up to the England U21 squad.

After finding himself behind Gordon Greer and Matthew Upson in the pecking order, Dunk had a brief loan spell with Bristol City in 2013, but re-established himself as first-choice centre-back during the 2014/15 season, finishing the season as top scorer and as runner-up to Inigo Calderon for the Player of the Season award.

Dunk played a pivotal role in Albion's 2016/17 promotion-winning season to the top tier as he formed an impressive partnership with Shane Duffy, and the pairing's understanding continued into Albion's debut season in the Premier League. The central-defender took up the role of vice captain, wearing the armband when Bruno was unavailable, and he scored his first Premier League goal against Arsenal at the Amex Stadium, as the Seagulls claimed a memorable 2-1 win.

Dunk played every single minute of Albion's 38 Premier League matches in 2017/18, as the Seagulls finished 15th and secured their top-flight status for another season.

He continued his impressive progress going into the 2018/19 season, and earned an historic first-ever call-up to the England squad for the UEFA Nations League matches against Croatia and Spain. Although Dunk's debut for Gareth Southgate's side did not arrive during that call-up, he made the following squad and won his first cap in a 3-0 victory over the USA at Wembley on 15 November 2018. His appearance in an England shirt made him the first Albion player since Steve Foster to win a full cap for the Three Lions.

Handed the Albion captaincy by new head coach Graham Potter ahead of the 2019/20 campaign, Dunk has remained a mainstay of the Albion defence and put pen-to-paper on a new five-year contract in August 2020 before captaining the side to a 16th-place finish last season.

LEWIS DUNK IN ACTION AGAINST WATFORD'S EMMANUEL DENNIS DURING THE 2-0 WIN AT THE AMEX, AUGUST 2021

ENGLAND'S LEWIS DUNK TACKLES USA'S CHRISTIAN PULISIC AT WEMBLEY, 2018

FULL NAME:	Lewis Carl Dunk
DATE OF BIRTH:	21 November 1991
PLACE OF BIRTH:	Brighton
POSITION:	Central defender

SEAGULLS APPEARANCES	SEAGULLS GOALS
343	**23**

LEAGUE:	313	LEAGUE:	20
FA CUP:	19	FA CUP:	1
LEAGUE CUP:	9	LEAGUE CUP:	1
OTHER:	2	OTHER:	1

ALBION DEBUT: MK Dons 0-0 Brighton & Hove Albion
1 May 2010 · League One

ALBION HONOURS: League One title winner 2010/11
Championship runner-up 2016/17
Player of the Season 2019/20

ENGLAND

APPEARANCES:	1	GOALS:	0

ENGLAND DEBUT: England 3-0 USA
15 November 2017

APPEARANCE AND GOALS CORRECT AS AT THE END OF 2020/21

49

REWIND
QUIZ OF THE YEAR

20 teasers to tackle on the Seagulls' 20/21 campaign...

With the Covid-19 pandemic resulting in the majority of the 2020/21 football season being played behind closed doors, what can you recall of the Seagulls' on-pitch action from the campaign?

1.

Albion played just two 2020/21 pre-season fixtures. Can you recall the two clubs they faced?

6.
Who scored the first and last goal of the club's 2020/21 League Cup campaign?

2.
From which club did the Seagulls sign Jakub Moder in October 2020?

4.
Can you name the summer signing who made his Albion debut in the opening game of the season at home to Chelsea?

7.
Against which club did Mathew Ryan record his first Premier League clean sheet in 2020/21?

9.
Brighton edged past Newport County on penalties in the third round of the FA Cup, but by what margin did they win the shoot-out?

3.
Who scored Brighton's first Premier League goal of 2020/21?

5.
Which south coast rival were Albion paired with in the EFL Cup?

8.
At what attempt did Brighton win their first Premier League home game of the 2020/21 season?

10.
Who were Albion's first opponents in the calendar year of 2021?

11. After featuring in all three of Albion's 2020/21 EFL Cup ties, which Championship side did Viktor Gyokeres join on a season-long loan in October 2020?

13. Who were the opposition when the Seagulls first welcomed 2,000 fans back to the Amex for a test event in December 2020?

16. Which two Premier League clubs did Albion record a double over in 2020/21?

12. Against which club did Danny Welbeck score his first Premier League goal for Brighton?

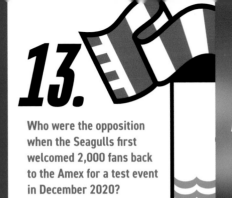

14. Albion recorded a memorable 1-0 victory away to Liverpool in February 2021, but before that, in which year was their last league triumph at Anfield?

15.

17. Who scored his first Albion goal to give the Seagulls a 3-2 victory over champions Manchester City in the final home game of the season?

19. With how many points did the Seagulls end their 2020/21 Premier League campaign?

Brighton bowed out of the FA Cup to the eventual winners in 2020/21. True or false?

18. How many different keepers did Brighton use in all competitions at first-team level during 2020/21?

20. Across their 2020/21 Premier League campaign, how many clean sheets did Albion manage to record?

ANSWERS ON PAGE 82

10 ALBION
YEARS AT THE AMEX

Mat Ryan
Goalkeeper

Mat RYAN

Australian international goalkeeper Mat Ryan was signed by Chris Hughton following the club's promotion to the Premier League in 2017.

Ryan agreed a five-year contract with the Seagulls in June 2017 and his Brighton debut coincided with the club's first match at Premier League level as the Amex hosted Manchester City on the opening day of the 2017/18 campaign.

Following his summer switch from Valencia, Ryan swiftly made his mark keeping ten clean sheets in an ever-present maiden campaign at the club. His performances helped win many valuable points across the season as the club secured its top-flight status. Across his 123 appearances for the Seagulls, Ryan won many plaudits for his impressive displays.

BRUNO

Right-back Bruno gained cult status at the Amex across a seven-season spell with the Seagulls.

Arriving in the summer of 2012 from Valencia, the experienced defender soon impressed with his enthusiasm and professionalism having a great impact on the squad. He was ever-present in the club's 2015/16 promotion near-miss and then featured in all bar four league games as the club sealed promotion from the Championship in 2016/17.

A key player as Albion established themselves at Premier League level, the popular Spaniard confirmed his retirement at the end of the 2018/19 season and has since joined the club's coaching staff.

Lewis DUNK

Brighton-born Lewis began his Seagulls career with the club still plying their trade at Withdean Stadium.

Dunk played in the very first competitive match at the Amex as the Seagulls overcame Doncaster Rovers in what was a memorable moment in Albion history. The reliable defender has since become a regular face at the heart of the Albion defence and a player synonymous with the success the club has enjoyed since moving to the Amex.

Currently club captain, Dunk is widely regarded as one of the best central defenders in the Premier League and his outstanding club form was recognised at international level when he won his first England cap in November 2018, in a friendly match against the USA at Wembley Stadium.

The Seagulls have boasted a wealth of talent over their ten years at the Amex! Here is our Brighton & Hove Albion DREAM TEAM ... see if you agree!

DREAM TEAM

BRUNO
Defender

Lewis **DUNK**
Defender

ALBION

53

ALBION DREAM TEAM

Matt UPSON
Defender

Shane DUFFY
Defender

54

Matt UPSON

Central defender Upson initially join Brighton on loan from Stoke City in January 2013.

Arriving at the Amex with over 20 full England caps to his name, he added a real touch of class and composure to Albion's defensive unit and was a star performer as the Seagulls reached the end-of-season Play-Offs in 2012/13.

Following the expiry of his contract at Stoke City, Upson delighted the Albion faithful when he agreed a permanent switch to the Amex in July 2013. Making 47 appearances in all competitions in Albion's 2013/14 Championship campaign, his polished performances won him the club's Player of the Season award.

Shane DUFFY

The big Irishman was a key figure in Albion's promotion to the Premier League and also in the years that have followed.

The centre-half has formed a key partnership with Lewis Dunk at the back and is a constant threat at set pieces.

While he initially fell out of favour following Graham Potter's arrival and spent last season on loan at Celtic, he returned to the Amex for 2021/22 with renewed focus and has been one of the side's star performers again.

Tariq LAMPTEY

England U21 international Lamptey has been a roaring success at the Amex Stadium following a January 2020 transfer from Chelsea.

A pacy right-sided defender who loves to get forward and support the attack, he has all the attributes to shine in the modern wing-back role.

The Covid-19 pandemic prevented Lamptey from showing the Amex faithful his skills in person, but with full crowds returning for the 2021/22 Premier League campaign, he is a player the home fans enjoy watching live. In January 2021, he agreed a new three-and-a-half-year deal with the Seagulls, ensuring his performances will light up the Amex for seasons to come.

David LOPEZ

Goalscoring midfielder David enjoyed two impressive seasons at the Amex after joining the Seagulls from Athletic Bilbao at the start of the 2012/13 campaign.

Earning the nickname 'Spanish Dave', he was a key player in the Albion side that twice reached the end-of-season Play-Offs during his time at the club.

He enjoyed a winning start to life at the Amex when he entered the fray in the final ten minutes of a 3-0 win over Sheffield Wednesday. His first Seagulls' goal came when he converted a late penalty to salvage a point against Millwall in December 2012. A popular character with fans and teammates, he made 71 Albion appearances, netting 12 goals.

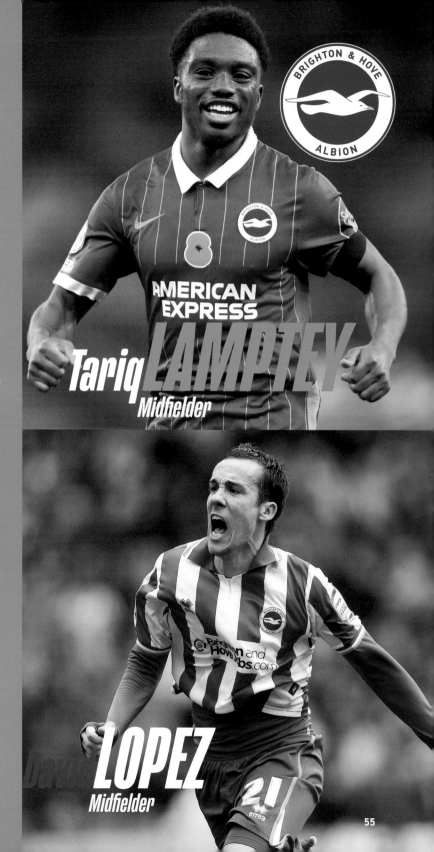

Tariq LAMPTEY
Midfielder

David LOPEZ
Midfielder

VICENTE
Midfielder

Anthony
KNOCKAERT
Midfielder

VICENTE

The Seagulls lured Spain international winger Vicente to the Amex in September 2011 following a lengthy and successful career in his homeland with Valencia where he won two La Liga titles.

A left footer with outstanding close control, pace and scoring ability, Vicente lit up the Amex and often had the crowd off their seats in anticipation of just what he might conjure up next.

Playing for the club across the first two seasons at the Amex, he made 32 appearances and netted five goals. He goes down in Albion folklore as one of the most exciting talents to wear the blue and white shirt.

Anthony KNOCKAERT

A star performer at the Amex, French winger Knockaert joined the Albion in January 2016 from Belgian side Standard Liege.

He wasted little time making his mark at the Amex and proved to be the real on-pitch driving force behind the Seagulls' 2016/17 promotion-winning campaign. In scintillating form throughout the season, Knockaert's 15 Championship goals and numerous assists saw him voted the Championship's Player of the Season.

He was also named Albion's Player of the Season at the conclusion of a memorable campaign that saw the club return to the top flight for the first time in 34 years.

Glenn MURRAY

Ace marksman Murray has enjoyed two goalscoring spells with Brighton and has twice sampled the joy of securing promotion with the Seagulls.

In his initial time at the club, he scored 22 goals in the Seagulls' 2010/11 League One title-winning season, ensuring the club began life at the Amex as a Championship side.

Murray again proved to be the focal point of the attack for Chris Hughton's side in 2016/17 and weighed in with 23 goals as Brighton secured promotion to the Premier League. The experienced frontman then excelled at Premier League level, netting a dozen goals in 2017/18 and then hitting 13 a season later.

Leonardo ULLOA

Powerful Argentinean striker Ulloa enjoyed a goalscoring debut for the Seagulls at the Amex.

Having joined the club from Almeria in the 2013 January transfer window, he soon impressed the Brighton crowd when he scored against Arsenal in the FA Cup.

In two seasons at the Amex, Ulloa boasted a highly impressive goal-to-games ratio with 26 goals from just 58 appearances between January 2013 and May 2014. During that period he took the mantle of becoming the first Albion player to net a hat-trick at the Amex Stadium when his treble helped secure a 4-1 victory over Huddersfield Town on 2 March 2013. His sensational scoring for the Seagulls resulted in a move to Leicester City in the summer of 2014.

ALBION DREAM TEAM

10 YEARS AT THE AMEX

BRIGHTON & HOVE ALBION

Glenn **MURRAY**
Striker

Leonardo **ULLOA**
Striker

57

The new season couldn't come quick enough for Albion fans and the excitement was fuelled further by the news that Manchester City would be the visitors on the opening day of the campaign. Chris Hughton looked to strengthen his squad by bringing in 11 new faces, the most notable being midfielders Pascal Gross and Davy Propper, goalkeeper Mat Ryan and winger Jose Izquierdo.

While City's team of superstars would go on to win the title with 100 points, starting with a 2-0 win at the Amex, Albion took plenty of belief from their own performance that day; as Lewis Dunk later said, "A learning experience against the very best."

Back-to-back games at Leicester City and Watford yielded just one point, picked up in a 0-0 draw at Vicarage Road, but there remained a real buzz of anticipation by the time West Brom arrived in Sussex after the international break.

The Baggies, under Tony Pulis, had made a bright start to the campaign, but were no match for the Seagulls who won 3-1, thanks to two Gross goals and a third from Tomer Hemed.

The opener came from the German shortly before the break when he converted Solly March's cross from close range – earning a place in the history books as Albion's first Premier League goalscorer and first in the top flight for 34 years. It was a win that gave Hughton's side renewed belief moving forward and a five-game unbeaten run through October and November saw the side hit the heady heights of eighth in the table.

The feelgood factor emanating around the club was further fuelled by a 2-1 FA Cup win against Crystal Palace in January, where Glenn Murray netted the winner three minutes from time against his former club. The cup run would continue well into spring, only to be ended in the sixth round at Manchester United.

Albion's Premier League status was, however, the key concern and three successive home wins in February and March, including a memorable 2-1 victory against Arsenal, went a long way to securing a place at the top table for another season.

Given such fortress-like form at the Amex, which also included a 1-1 draw against Tottenham in mid-April, it was somewhat apt that safety was secured with a win in Sussex against Manchester United in early May. Gross was again the man of the moment, netting the game's solitary goal in the 57th minute.

Albion finished their debut Premier League campaign in a more than respectable 15th place and had hit the fabled 40-point mark, some seven points clear of danger.

PASCAL GROSS SCORES THE SEAGULLS' FIRST PREMIER LEAGUE GOAL V WBA

BRIGHTON & HOVE ALBION

10 YEARS AT THE AMEX

2017/18

JOSE IZQUIERDO DURING THE 1-0 WIN OVER MANCHESTER UNITED, MAY 2018

MANAGER: *Chris Hughton*

LEAGUE: *Premier League*

FINAL LEAGUE POSITION: *15th*

TOP SCORER: *Glenn Murray (14 IN ALL COMPETITIONS*

LEAGUE WINS: *9*

LEAGUE GOALS SCORED: *34*

LEAGUE POINTS WON: *40*

AVERAGE HOME ATTENDANCE: *30,392*

PLAYER OF THE SEASON: *Pascal Gross*

SHANE DUFFY CELEBRATES SCORING THE SECOND GOAL AGAINST MANCHESTER UNITED, AUGUST 2018

MANAGER: *Chris Hughton*

LEAGUE: *Premier League*

FINAL LEAGUE POSITION: **17th**

TOP SCORER: *Glenn Murray*
(15 IN ALL COMPETITIONS)

LEAGUE WINS: **9**

LEAGUE GOALS SCORED: **35**

LEAGUE POINTS WON: **36**

AVERAGE HOME ATTENDANCE: **30,426**

PLAYER OF THE SEASON: *Shane Duffy*

2018/19

KNOCKAERT CELEBRATES HIS WINNER AT SELHURST PARK MARCH 2019

We often hear of a 'second season syndrome' afflicting Premier League newcomers, so all eyes were on Chris Hughton's men to see if they could steer themselves clear of danger for a second successive campaign.

There was a flurry of transfer activity pre-season, with recruitment largely focused on the continent: Martin Montoya, Alireza Jahanbakhsh, Leon Balogun, Florin Andone, Bernardo and Yves Bissouma all putting pen to paper. A 2-0 opening-day defeat at Watford would have been an eye-opener to the newcomers present, with Manchester United next on the agenda.

Would history repeat itself? Could the Seagulls repeat their match-winning performance at the end of the previous campaign? The answer was a resounding yes as Glenn Murray, Shane Duffy and a Pascal Gross penalty handed the hosts an impressive 3-1 lead at half time. While Paul Pogba netted from the spot in the 90th minute, the display was more dominant than the scoreline suggested.

Albion failed to build on the momentum, however, and were winless from their next five league games, so back-to-back 1-0 home wins against West Ham and Wolves – sandwiching another single-goal victory at Newcastle United – would prove crucial to the campaign. Victory against the Molineux club also witnessed Glenn Murray's 100th goal for the club – the second man to reach the milestone behind Tommy Cook.

Albion's form remained streaky; back-to-back wins against Huddersfield and Crystal Palace in early December – the latter a 3-1 win with ten men for more than an hour of the game – were tempered by successive defeats against Burnley, Chelsea and Bournemouth. Still, a 1-0 home win against Everton at the turn of the year left the side in 13th place and a sizeable points gap with the bottom three remained.

The second half of the campaign, though, proved particularly difficult, with just two league wins picked up from January to May. One of those victories will be talked about for years to come; a 2-1 win at rivals Palace which not only secured a league double against the Eagles but also witnessed a superb curling winner from Anthony Knockaert, which inevitably won the club's Goal of the Season.

The FA Cup proved to be a welcome distraction with Bournemouth, West Brom, Derby and Millwall all defeated, to set up a Wembley semi-final encounter against Manchester City. The Citizens started as clear favourites, but only a solitary Gabriel Jesus goal separated the sides in front of over 71,000 fans.

Back-to-back draws against Arsenal and Newcastle United ensured Albion's status was assured by the time City again faced the Seagulls on the final day of the season. The game would prove far more memorable for the opposition though, with Pep Guardiola's men coming from behind to win 4-1, securing a second successive Premier League title.

59

AMERICAN EXPRE

ELITE FOOTBALL

PERFORMANCE

PREMIER 2 LEAGUE

BACK ROW (L-R): Tom Ball, Ed Turns, Lars Dendoncker, Harry Wood, Odel Offiah, Evan Ferguson, Antef Tsoungui, Jack Pugh.

MIDDLE ROW: Jamie Gillett, Jeremy Sarmiento, Laurent Tolaj, Ben Wilson, Adam Desbois, Fynn Talley, Tom McGill, Marc Leonard, Matt Everitt, Todd Miller, James Hamilton.

FRONT ROW: Cameron Peupion, James Furlong, Ayo Tanimowo, Shannon Ruth, Andrew Crofts, Gary Dicker, Jack Spong, Andrew Moran, Sam Packham.

ENTRE

TOBY BULL

POSITION Goalkeeper   **DOB:** 23/08/2003

Eighteen-year-old goalkeeper Bull progressed through the age groups within the club's academy set-up. He gained useful experience when he spent time out on loan with local Isthmian Premier League club Worthing in the 2020/21 season. He also played nine times for the U18s last season, including a run of three clean sheets in a seven-match unbeaten run in the league. The 2020/21 campaign also saw Bull feature for the U17 side who enjoyed success in the Premier League Cup where they defeated their Middlesbrough counterparts in the final.

ADAM DESBOIS

POSITION: Goalkeeper   **DOB:** 05/01/2001

Another talented young goalkeeper among the Seagulls' academy ranks, Desbois joined the Albion from Reading in 2019. An impressive 'keeper who has demonstrated great reflexes and confident handling skills since arriving at the American Express Elite Football Performance Centre. The 20-year-old received international recognition when he was called into the England U17 squad during his time with the Royals. Desbois made his debut for Albion's U23s during the 2020/21 campaign in a 2-2 draw with Everton and will be keen for more action at Premier League 2 level throughout the 2021/22 campaign.

LARS DENDONCKER

POSITION: Defender   **DOB:** 03/04/2001

Belgian central defender Dendoncker agreed a two-year deal with the Albion in August 2020 and linked up with the club's U23 squad in 2020/21. The younger brother of Wolves star Leander, Lars joined the Seagulls from the Club Brugge youth team. Extremely comfortable in possession, he can also operate in a defensive midfield role if called upon. The 20-year-old will continue his development in 2021/22 with a season-long loan at Scottish Premier League side St Johnstone.

GARY DICKER

POSITION Midfielder   **DOB:** 31/07/1986

Dicker returned to Brighton in July 2021 to take up the role of coach/over-age player in the U23 squad. The 34-year-old midfielder made 153 appearances for the club after joining in March 2009 on loan from Stockport County. He made the move permanent that July and spent the next four seasons with the club. After spells with Rochdale, Crawley Town and Carlisle United, he joined Scottish Premiership side Kilmarnock in 2016, making more than 150 appearances and coaching the reserve team for four years before he was released at the end of last season.

ULRICK ELLA

POSITION Forward   DOB: 22/05/2001

Ella joined the Albion in September 2020 from Ligue 2 side Amiens. He is a French U19 international who can operate either as a forward or a winger. Having progressed through the youth ranks at Lens and Auxerre, he joined the academy at Austrian side FC Salzburg in 2017, who loaned him to their fellow Red Bull club FC Liefering in 2019. He returned to France when he joined Amiens in the summer of 2019, and he has been capped by France at U16 to U19 level.

EVAN FERGUSON

POSITION: Forward   DOB: 19/10/2004

A towering centre-forward, Ferguson joined Brighton from Bohemians in January 2021. He has already been capped by the Republic of Ireland at U21 level and had a brief taste of first-team action with Albion – and all before his 17th birthday. The teenager made an instant impression upon his arrival as he netted three goals in 11 Premier League 2 outings. Ferguson's first-team debut arrived alongside a number of his academy teammates when he featured as a substitute in a youthful Seagulls side that defeated Cardiff City in the second round of the League Cup in August 2021.

MATT EVERITT

POSITION: Forward   DOB: 24/10/2002

An attacking midfielder, Everitt joined the Brighton & Hove Albion academy set-up from Brentford back in 2016. He captained the U18s regularly during the 2020/21 season and is one of a host of exciting young talents who will now step up to show their worth at U23 level in Premier League 2 this season. The teenager has also been capped by the Republic of Ireland at both U17 and U19 level.

JAMES FURLONG

POSITION Defender   DOB: 07/06/2003

Dublin-born left-back Furlong linked up with the Albion academy when he joined the club from Shamrock Rovers in the summer of 2019. The teenager's club form has won him international recognition with the Republic of Ireland at U18 level. After impressing for the Seagulls' U18 side, he made his debut for the U23 development team in September 2020. Very much the modern full-back, Furlong likes to foray forward and support attacks, but has the ability to combine his forward runs while maintaining his defensive responsibilities.

JACK HINCHY

POSITION Midfielder   **DOB:** 16/06/2002

Hinchy signed for Brighton from National League side Stockport County and agreed a two-year deal in August 2021.
He arrived at the Albion having made his first-team debut for the Hatters in January 2021, in a narrow 1-0 home defeat in an FA Cup third round tie at home to West Ham United. His experience gained in the National League will certainly serve the midfielder well as he now continues his development in Premier League 2.

TOM McGILL

POSITION: Goalkeeper   **DOB:** 25/03/2000

McGill joined Albion at 14 years of age and has represented England at U17 level. He progressed through the club's youth ranks, before joining the U23 squad for the 2018/19 campaign. The goalkeeper made over 30 appearances for Albion's U18s in the Premier League South, and made a loan move to Greenwich Borough during his first season as an U23 squad member. Priceless first-team experience has since been gained with loan spells at Basingstoke Town and Crawley Town.

ANDREW MORAN

POSITION Midfielder   **DOB:** 15/10/2003

The calendar year of 2021 has certainly been eventful for midfielder Moran who initially joined the Albion academy from Bray Wanderers in 2020. His impressive performance for the U18s in 2020/21 saw him make a handful of appearances for the U23s in his debut season and in July 2021 he signed his first professional contract with the club. Already this season he has made his debut for the Republic of Ireland U21s and tasted first-team action for the Seagulls – coming off the bench in the 2-0 League Cup victory over Cardiff City in August.

MARC LEONARD

POSITION: Midfielder   **DOB:** 19/12/2001

Goalscoring midfielder Leonard joined the Albion from Scottish club Heart of Midlothian in 2018. Playing regularly in the U18s, he was promoted to the U23s squad for the 2020/21 season. The youngster impressed at this level in the opening weeks of the 2021/22 campaign with three goals and one assist from his first four appearances of the season. His progress was further rewarded with a full first-team debut in August 2021 as Brighton defeated Cardiff City in the second round of the League Cup.

TODD MILLER

POSITION Forward   **DOB:** 01/10/2002

Tricky winger Miller began his youth career with Dagenham & Redbridge before moving on to Colchester United at the age of 14. In March 2019 he was called into the United first-team squad and made his professional debut in a League Two match away to Exeter City on 16 March 2019. Aged 16 years and 166 days at the time of his U's debut, Miller is the Essex club's youngest player. He joined Brighton in the summer of 2019 and agreed a three-year deal before linking up with the U23 development squad.

ODEL OFFIAH

POSITION: Defender   **DOB:** 30/12/2002

Offiah progressed through the ranks with non-league Bromley, before joining the Albion academy in 2017. Born in Camden, he is the nephew of former Rugby League and Rugby Union star Martin Offiah MBE. The powerful centre back moved up to the U18s in 2019 and was one of a number of youngsters that was handed a first-team debut by head coach Graham Potter in the Seagulls' League Cup tie at Cardiff City in August 2021. He got his first taste of professional action as he replaced Taylor Richards in the 68th minute of Brighton's 2-0 cup triumph in South Wales.

SAM PACKHAM

POSITION Defender   **DOB:** 08/11/2001

Versatile defender Packham has been with the Albion academy since he was eight years old. The Redhill-born teenager has progressed though the age groups and he put pen-to-paper on a first professional contract, together with teammate Ayo Tanimowo, in July 2020, following an impressive season for the U18s side. Packham made his first appearance for the U23s in a 2-2 draw with Arsenal in September 2020 and began the new 2021/22 campaign as a regular performer for Andrew Crofts' team in Premier League 2.

JEREMY SARMIENTO

POSITION: Forward   **DOB:** 16/06/2002

Sarmiento was a summer 2021 signing from Portuguese side Benfica. The exciting forward joined the Seagulls on a two-year deal and links up with the club's U23 development squad. The former England U17 international came through the ranks with Charlton Athletic before signing for Benfica in 2018. A player blessed with flair and technical ability, His infectious appetite for the game and willingness to learn has already won him praise from U23's head coach Andrew Crofts. He made his senior debut in the League Cup win against Swansea in September.

FYNN TALLEY

POSITION Goalkeeper   **DOB:** 19/09/2002

Teenage goalkeeper Talley joined the Albion academy from Premier League rivals Arsenal in 2017. He went on loan to Isthmian League South East Division outfit Burgess Hill Town in January 2020, before returning to Brighton and featuring regularly for the club's U18 side the following season. His performances at U18 level certainly impressed the Seagulls' coaching staff and the former Gunner was rewarded with a first professional contract in July 2020. He will be looking to establish himself in Andrew Crofts' U23 team in 2021/22.

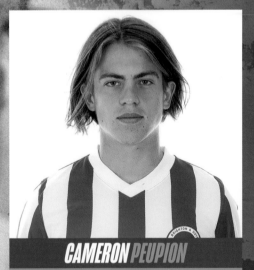

CAMERON PEUPION

POSITION: Midfielder   **DOB:** 23/09/2002

Peupion joined Albion from Sydney FC in August 2020 and spent his first season on the south coast in the U18s side. Following a number of eye-catching performances throughout the 2020/21 campaign, the Australian teenager has stepped up to Andrew Crofts' U23 development squad for the 2021/22 campaign.
Peupion wasted little time in making his mark at U23 level as he added his name to the scoresheet on his debut as the Seagulls defeated their Derby Country counterparts 2-0 in Premier League 2.

JACK SPONG

POSITION: Midfielder   **DOB:** 04/02/2002

Spong has progressed through the Albion academy and has already had a brief taste of first-team football to his name. Having been a regular in the U18 side throughout the 2018/19 season, he was ready for the challenge of stepping up to the U23s in the summer of 2019 but found himself thrust into the limelight when he was handed a professional debut in the Seagulls' League Cup meeting with Aston Villa at the Amex in September 2019. After appearing from the bench against Villa, he has continued his progress in the U23 development squad.

AYO TANIMOWO

POSITION: Defender   **DOB:** 09/11/2001

Right-back Tanimowo joined the Seagulls' academy from Norwich City in 2018 and the 19-year-old spent his first two years with Albion in the U18s. A speedy full-back who loves to get forward and support the attack, he is an excellent defender in one-on-one situations and was rewarded with a first professional contract in July 2020. He progressed to the U23 side in the summer of 2020 and made 19 appearances in the club's 2020/21 Premier League 2 campaign.

LORENT TOLAJ

POSITION: Forward **DOB:** 23/10/2001

A Switzerland U19 international forward, Tolaj joined the Albion academy back in 2018 and made headlines when he scored seven times for his country in a match against Gibraltar U19s. Tolaj suffered an injury-hit 2020/21 campaign with knee and hamstring problems resulting in him making just two appearances for the U23s at the tail-end of last season. The teenager will be hoping for better luck in 2021/22 and started the new season in fine form with his first goal of the campaign coming in Brighton's comprehensive 4-1 victory over Blackburn Rovers in Premier League 2.

ED TURNS

POSITION Defender **DOB:** 18/10/2002

Central-defender Turns has progressed through the Albion academy system, making his U18s debut in the 2018/19 season. The left-footed centre-back brings excellent balance to a defensive unit and made his debut for the U23 development side in Premier League 2 in October 2020. After a number of outings at U23 level last season, the opening weeks of the current 2021/22 season have seen Turns establish himself as a regular face in Andrew Crofts' side. He was rewarded with a senior debut against Swansea in the League Cup in September, playing the full 90 minutes in the 2-0 win.

ANTEF TSOUNGUI

POSITION Defender **DOB:** 30/12/2002

Defender Tsoungui spent time in the youth ranks with Chelsea before joining Albion's academy in the summer of 2018. He swiftly progressed through the youth system on the south coast, going on to play regularly in the U18s and U23s, before being handed a first-team opportunity by Graham Potter at the start of the current campaign. Tsoungui's professional bow came in the 2-0 League Cup victory away to Cardiff City in August 2021 when he took his place in a youthful Seagulls line-up.

BEN WILSON

POSITION: Forward **DOB:** 05/12/2001

Pacy frontman Wilson will be looking to make up for lost time in 2021/22 after injuries curtailed his development last season. Handed the timely boost of a one-year contract extension in the summer of 2021, the former Coleraine man will be keen to show his undoubted potential after a hamstring problem was followed by a training ground injury, resulting in the need for major hip surgery. The Derry-born forward is expected to be back in action for Andrew Crofts' U23 development side before the end of the calendar year.

PREMIER 2 LEAGUE

Chris Hughton's memorable reign as Albion boss had come to an end following the final kick of the 2018/19 season, with the club's board seeking a change of direction in terms of style and substance.

Former Ostersunds and Swansea City coach Graham Potter was appointed in late May, and while his appointment might have raised eyebrows outside of BN1, there was widespread approval from the playing squad, who clearly enjoyed the style of play adopted in pre-season. That aesthetically-pleasing approach was also in evidence on the opening day as a 3-5-2 formation was adopted for a comprehensive 3-0 win at Watford. On target was Neal Maupay, who joined Leandro Trossard and Adam Webster as new faces added to the squad.

Home fans got a taste of the new era for the visit of West Ham United; a game where VAR – in operation at the stadium in the Premier League for the first time – denied debutant Trossard an opening goal. The Belgian didn't have to wait long, though, to make his mark as he netted a 65th minute equaliser in a 1-1 draw.

With a new ethos, it inevitably took time for the players to find their feet, which resulted in a six-game winless league run. Potter was also happy to blood players from the U23 set-up, with Aaron Connolly and Steven Alzate stepping up, while nine academy players featured in a Carabao Cup defeat against Aston Villa.

Connolly emerged as the star of the show as Albion picked up a spectacular second league win of the season, a 3-0 defeat of Champions League finalists Tottenham Hotspur in late October, with the young Irishman netting a goal in each half. Successive home victories followed against Everton and Norwich City to further increase Potter's stock as his side sat eighth in the table.

Other highlights of the opening half of the season included another north London scalp, with Arsenal beaten 2-1 win at the Emirates in early December, while Chelsea were held 1-1 at the Amex on New Year's Day – the highlight being a superb overhead kick by Alireza Jahanbakhsh.

Away from football there was concern mounting with the COVID-19 pandemic taking a hold throughout Europe. By the time Arsenal were set to visit in March, Gunners boss Mikel Arteta had tested positive for coronavirus, sparking a chain of events that would see football postponed indefinitely.

After 105 days on the sidelines, it was a very different environment that greeted Albion's return against Arsenal. Yet for Albion fans watching from home, there was unbridled joy as Neal Maupay's last-gasp winner set the tone for an impressive return to action that saw the club retain its place in the Premier League with a club record top-flight tally of 41 points, thanks in part to further wins against Norwich and Burnley.

BRIGHTON & HOVE ALBION

10 YEARS AT THE AMEX

AARON CONNOLLY CELEBRATES HIS FIRST GOAL V SPURS, OCTOBER 2019

AMERICAN EXPRESS

2019/20

LEWIS DUNK CONGRATULATES NEAL MAUPAY ON HIS GOAL V WATFORD

MAUPAY 7

HEAD COACH: *Graham Potter*

LEAGUE: *Premier League*

FINAL LEAGUE POSITION: **15th**

TOP SCORER: *Neal Maupay* (10 IN ALL COMPETITIONS)

LEAGUE WINS: **9**

LEAGUE GOALS SCORED: **39**

LEAGUE POINTS WON: **41**

AVERAGE HOME ATTENDANCE: **22,369** (30,350 pre-COV)

PLAYER OF THE SEASON: *Lewis Dunk*

STEVEN ALZATE CELEBRATES
SCORING THE ONLY GOAL AGAINST
LIVERPOOL WITH NEAL MAUPAY

With the nation still in the grip of the COVID-19 pandemic, the new season saw games continue to be played behind closed doors.

Albion had made a number of impressive signings with internationals Danny Welbeck, Joel Veltman and Adam Lallana joining the ranks, and while the campaign began with a 3-1 home defeat against Chelsea, the side soon got back on track with a comprehensive 3-0 win at Newcastle United.

It teed the players up nicely for the visit of Manchester United in late September, a controversial game which saw Solly March net a 95th minute goal to make it 2-2, only for Bruno Fernandes to score a VAR-assisted penalty in the 110th minute – after referee Chris Kavanagh had blown for full-time. Albion also hit the woodwork five times: a Premier League record.

It was a game that typified Albion's season; a rollercoaster ride, with some wonderful highs, frustrating lows and plenty of good football played along the way. The general opinion was that, over the course of the campaign, the club hadn't picked up the points tally the performances deserved – highlighted by the fact that just four Amex league wins were registered all season.

The players were clearly missing the raucous atmosphere generated when the Amex is full, although prior to the winter lockdown, some 2,000 fans had been present for the visits of Southampton and Sheffield United.

A first home win came as late as 31 January, with Leandro Trossard netting as Tottenham left empty-handed for a second successive season. Those three points teed up, arguably, the club's greatest ever league victory, a 1-0 win at champions Liverpool three days later, thanks to Steven Alzate's 56th minute goal.

February was also a month which witnessed Albion's most frustrating defeat of the season – a 2-1 home reverse against Crystal Palace, in which the visitors netted a 90th minute winner on the back of the following statistics: 74.5% Albion possession, 25 shots to the Eagles' three and 13 corners to zero.

WELBECK'S GOAL OF THE SEASON AGAINST LEEDS UNITED

Another late defeat to Leicester City in early March left the Seagulls sitting uncomfortably just three points ahead of 18th placed Fulham – but back-to-back wins at Southampton [2-1] and at home to Leeds United [2-0], where Welbeck netted the side's Goal of the Season with a tremendous turn and shot, all but secured Albion's top-flight status for another season.

By the time champions Manchester City visited for the penultimate game of the season, safety was assured. It was time for celebration; not just because a record-breaking fifth season of top-flight football had been secured, but because almost 8,000 fans were allowed back into the stadium to witness the 3-2 win as lockdown rules eased, with hopes of more fans to follow come August.

HEAD COACH: *Graham Potter*

LEAGUE: *Premier League*

FINAL LEAGUE POSITION: *16th*

TOP SCORER: *Neal Maupay*
(8 IN ALL COMPETITIONS)

LEAGUE WINS: *9*

LEAGUE GOALS SCORED: *40*

LEAGUE POINTS WON: *41*

AVERAGE HOME ATTENDANCE: *629*
(3,982 EX. BEHIND CLOSED DOORS)

PLAYER OF THE SEASON: *Ben White*

2020/21

2020/21 PREMIER LEAGUE HIGHLIGHTS

NEWCASTLE UNITED 0-3 BRIGHTON & HOVE ALBION

ALBION SCORERS: *MAUPAY 2, CONNOLLY*

Neal Maupay bagged a brace as Albion put in a dominant performance to pick up their first Premier League win of the season. The striker opened his account in the fourth minute from the penalty spot after the impressive Tariq Lamptey had been fouled by Allan Saint-Maximin. He then doubled his account just three minutes later when he finished off a move down the right involving Lamptey and Leandro Trossard. Maupay's strike partner, Aaron Connolly, then put the icing on the cake seven minutes from time when he coolly curled the ball home.

"The three points were the most important thing. I thought we played some good football at times, dug deep when we had to, but it was a good win – we deserved it." **TARIQ LAMPTEY**

SEPTEMBER

CRYSTAL PALACE 1-1 BRIGHTON & HOVE ALBION

PALACE SCORER: *ZAHA* **ALBION SCORER:** *MAC ALLISTER*

Albion picked up a deserved point at Selhurst Park thanks to Alexis Mac Allister's late strike. The Seagulls had their rivals on the back foot for much of the game, but it was Palace who took the lead from the penalty spot when Tariq Lamptey was adjudged to have dragged down Michy Batshuayi – even though replays showed there was little contact on the Palace striker. Wilfried Zaha converted, which proved to be the home side's only shot on target, but the Seagulls were all smiles in the 90th minute when the Argentine latched on to fellow sub Aaron Connolly's lay-off, to drill home a rasping first-time effort.

"It was a beautiful day because in Argentina it was Mother's Day and I dedicated my goal to my mum. She is one of the most important people in my life – I love her and miss her." **ALEXIS MAC ALLISTER**

OCTOBER

ASTON VILLA 1-2 BRIGHTON & HOVE ALBION

VILLA SCORER: *KONZA* **ALBION SCORERS:** *WELBECK, MARCH*

NOVEMBER

The Seagulls picked up their first-ever win at Villa Park, deservedly edging a thriller which also had a dramatic ending. Danny Welbeck netted his first goal for the club when he latched on to Adam Lallana's delightful poke forward before cleverly lifting the ball over Emi Martinez in the Villa goal. Ezri Konza grabbed an equaliser shortly after the restart, sliding in from close range, before Solly March netted a superb goal when he curled home with his right foot from 18 yards. There was injury-time drama when March challenged Trezeguet inside the box, and referee Michael Oliver pointed to the spot. However, he reversed his decision having consulted the touchline monitor.

"We've had a few penalties against us this season so I'm not sure what is and what isn't a penalty these days. I know Solly touched the ball so we're just happy it went our way this time." **GRAHAM POTTER**

BRIGHTON & HOVE ALBION 1-2 SOUTHAMPTON

ALBION SCORER: *GROSS* **SOUTHAMPTON SCORERS:** *VESTERGAARD, INGS (PEN)*

While Albion were undone by a controversial VAR decision, this fixture was all about the fans – back at the Amex for the first time in the Premier League since February. While numbers were limited to 2,000 they still made a din and got behind the side from start to finish. Albion took the lead through Pascal Gross' penalty, after James Ward-Prowse had handled, but the visitors equalised through Jannik Vestergaard's powerful header. Saints won the game from the penalty spot when Solly March was adjudged to have brought down Kyle Walker-Peters, with referee David Coote initially blowing for a free-kick.

"The result was frustrating, especially the way we lost. It was great to have the fans back though. It has been a long time without them." **SOLLY MARCH**

DECEMBER

BRIGHTON & HOVE ALBION 1-0 TOTTENHAM HOTSPUR

ALBION SCORER: TROSSARD

With the momentum of a three-game unbeaten run behind them, including an impressive 1-0 win at Leeds, the Seagulls put in a complete performance to beat their Champions League-chasing opponents and record a first home win of the season in the league. Albion were on the front foot throughout the game, created the better chances, and took a deserved three points when Leandro Trossard side-footed home a Pascal Gross cross. Gareth Bale also headed a Lewis Dunk effort off the line while Ben White and Aaron Connolly had chances to extend the lead in the second half.

"It's true a home win has been a long time coming, so we're pleased to have finally done it now. We are also really pleased with the way we played, against a top side." PASCAL GROSS

LIVERPOOL 0-1 BRIGHTON & HOVE ALBION

ALBION SCORER: ALZATE

Wednesday 3 February 2021 is a date that will leave an indelible mark on Albion's long history: the day when Liverpool, the current Premier League champions, were beaten in their own backyard by the Seagulls for the first time in the top flight since 1982. Coming just three days after the impressive win against Tottenham, the momentum continued at Anfield as the side put in a performance of real courage and endeavour. It was also a controlled and disciplined performance, as the Reds searched to cancel out Steven Alzate's deflected effort - his first Premier League goal for the Seagulls.

"We fought when we had to – we had to block and defend as a team – but I thought we showed quality when we attacked and courage and bravery with the ball. To come here and get the result we have, I think you have got to be close to perfect. I thought we were." GRAHAM POTTER

BRIGHTON & HOVE ALBION 3-0 NEWCASTLE UNITED

ALBION SCORERS: TROSSARD, WELBECK, MAUPAY

It was a game billed in some quarters as a 'six pointer' as both sides knew victory would pull them clear of 18th-placed Fulham - and it was the Albion who extended their gap over the Cottagers to six points following a dominant display. On the front foot from the first whistle, the Seagulls took the lead in first-half stoppage time when Leandro Trossard delightfully curled the ball home. Albion's second, shortly after the restart, was every bit as good as Danny Welbeck netted from distance, while Neal Maupay put the icing on the cake when he met a Pascal Gross cross to net his eighth goal of the season.

"It looked like a carbon copy of Leandro's goal, but believe me it wasn't something that was planned. As strikers, we work on different finishes and the space opened up for me." DANNY WELBECK

CHELSEA 0-0 BRIGHTON & HOVE ALBION

In a game delayed for 15 minutes by the anti-European Super League protests outside Stamford Bridge, Albion went toe-to-toe with the eventual Champions League winners. Yet again, the Seagulls were brave in possession at one of the top clubs in the country and could well have come away with all three points. Adam Lallana missed a good chance from close range while a Danny Welbeck whipped effort from distance came back off a post. The point moved Albion seven points clear of the drop zone.

"It's so hard to get points in this league, so we have to be happy. It could have been more but we'll take it." ADAM WEBSTER

BRIGHTON & HOVE ALBION 3-2 MANCHESTER CITY

ALBION SCORERS: TROSSARD, WEBSTER, BURN   CITY SCORERS: GUNDOGAN, FODEN

In a game that welcomed not only the newly-crowned champions but 8,000 fans to the Amex, the match got off to the worst possible start, with Ilkay Gundogan netting after two minutes. There was a glimmer of hope, however, on ten minutes when Joao Cancelo was red-carded for bringing down Danny Welbeck. It appeared not to concern the visitors, who extended their lead shortly after the break through a fine individual Phil Foden goal. Yet within two minutes, the fightback had begun: Leandro Trossard netted and with the momentum in their favour, Adam Webster and Dan Burn scored to record a memorable victory.

"I've been waiting a long time for a Premier League goal. I've had a few cancelled out by VAR and to be honest I thought I might have been offside when I scored so I was delighted it went over the line." DAN BURN

69

PREMIER LEAGUE QUIZ

20 TEASERS TO TACKLE ON THE 2021/22 PREMIER LEAGUE CLUBS

6.

Romelu Lukaku joined Chelsea for a second time in August 2021 when he signed from Inter Milan, but which club did he leave to first join the Blues in 2011?

1.

Ahead of which Premier League season did Arsenal move to the Emirates Stadium?

2.

Prior to this summer's record signing of Emi Buendia from Norwich City, who was Aston Villa's previous record signing?

4.

At which venue did Brighton & Hove Albion play a competitive league fixture for the first time in 2021/22?

7.

Crystal Palace manager Patrick Vieira is famed for his playing career with Arsenal, but which other Premier League side has Vieira played for?

Who was the last man to manage Leeds United in the Premier League before Marcelo Bielsa?

9.

3.

Brentford are competing in the Premier League for the first time in 2021/22, but when were the Bees last in the top flight?

5.

With which country has Burnley striker Chris Wood won over fifty international caps?

8.

Prior to Dominic Calvert-Lewin, who was the last Everton player to score for England?

10.

How many other current Premier League clubs has Leicester City boss Brendan Rodgers managed?

11.

From which club did Liverpool sign the Premier League goalscoring sensation Mohamed Salah?

12.

Who scored the dramatic late final-day goal that won Manchester City their first Premier League title in 2011/12?

13.

Can you name the Manchester United and England U21 international full-back who has been loaned to a Premier League club for 2021/22?

14.

Newcastle's summer signing Joe Willock enjoyed a successful loan spell at St James' Park before joining the Magpies permanently.

How many Premier League goals did Willock score while on loan last season - 8, 9 or 10?

15.

Prior to Daniel Farke, who was the last manager to guide Norwich City to promotion to the Premier League?

16.

Southampton signed striker Adam Armstrong from Blackburn Rovers ahead of the 2021/22 season, but at which Premier League club did he begin his career?

17.

Other than Spurs, which other club has Harry Kane played Premier League football for?

18.

During Watford's last Premier League campaign in 2019/20, how many different managers did the Hornets have?

19.

Can you name the current Match of the Day pundit who scored his last Premier League goal for West Ham United?

20.

Prior to Conor Coady who was Wolves' last Premier League player to play for England?

ANSWERS ON PAGE 82

71

ALBION U18s

BACK ROW: Samy Chouchane, Zak Sturge, Leigh Kavanagh, Ben Jackson, Casper Nilsson, Marcus Ifill.

MIDDLE ROW: Calum Brashill, Eliot Jenks, Ruairi McConville, Tommy Reid, Hugo Fisher, Joshua Duffus, Jack Hinshelwood, Rianna Farr.

FRONT ROW: Justinas Gasiunas, Bailey Smith, Jake Gee, Joe Winstanley, Jaami Qureshi, John Lucero, James Baxter.

JOSHUA DUFFUS

POSITION: Centre Forward
DATE OF BIRTH: 31/05/2005

A very energetic striker who knows where the back of the net is. Hails from south London and had a spell at Crystal Palace before he joined the Albion at the foundation phase age group.

HUGO FISHER

POSITION: Goalkeeper
DATE OF BIRTH: 24/09/2004

Slovakian-born goalkeeper, he was spotted playing grassroots football and has been with the club's academy since the foundation phase. A very good shot-stopper, he originally hails from Croydon.

JAKE GEE

POSITION: Centre Midfield
DATE OF BIRTH: 04/09/2004

Released by Fulham, he has arrived at the Albion with the reputation of being a very creative midfielder. He is a good technical player who often plays in the number 10 role.

ELIOT JENKS

POSITION: Centre Midfield
DATE OF BIRTH: 20/10/2004

Younger brother of Albion U23 player Teddy, Eliot is another player who has been with the club since the age of eight. He is a box-to-box combative midfielder who, like Jack, is not afraid of a tackle.

RUAIRI McCONVILLE

POSITION: Centre Back
DATE OF BIRTH: 01/05/2005

A player who has joined the club from Linfield in Northern Ireland, he is a ball-playing centre-half. He is the U17 captain for his country and signed after a successful trial.

TOMMY REID

POSITION: Goalkeeper
DATE OF BIRTH: 18/01/2005

Having come right through the academy system, he has represented England at U15 and U16 levels. A very good distributor of the ball with both feet and hands.

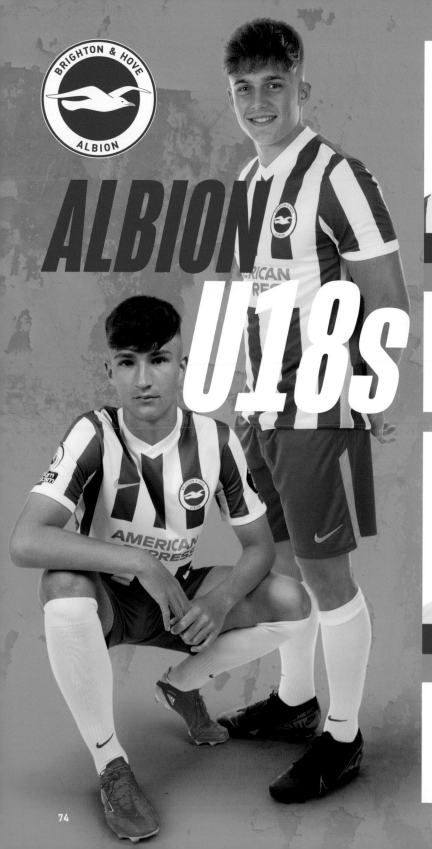

ALBION *U18s*

BAILEY *SMITH*

POSITION: Right Wing
DATE OF BIRTH: 02/05/2005

A local lad from Worthing, he is a very quick and direct player. He could have become an athlete, ranked as one of the top-five quickest 200m runners in the country at his age group.

JOE *WINSTANLEY*

POSITION: Right Back
DATE OF BIRTH: 01/11/2004

Signed this summer from Wigan Athletic, he is a very hard-working and energetic full-back. He has played for England at U15 level.

TOBIAS *COLLYER*

POSITION: Centre Midfield
DATE OF BIRTH: 03/01/2004

Arrived at U10 level. A local lad from Worthing, he has represented England at U15, U17 and U19 levels. Very comfortable on the ball as a deep-lying midfielder.

ZAK *EMMERSON*

POSITION: Centre Forward
DATE OF BIRTH: 12/08/2004

Signed from Oldham Athletic in the summer of 2020, he is a centre-forward who is equally good getting in behind or with the ball at his feet. He played for Oldham's first team before making the move south.

MARCUS IFILL

POSITION: Right Wing/Centre Forward
DATE OF BIRTH: 02/11/2003

Scored in the 2-0 Premier League U17 cup final win against Middlesbrough last season. He joined the Albion at U16 level from Swindon Town and is a rapid winger who can also play through the middle.

BENJAMIN JACKSON

POSITION: Centre Back
DATE OF BIRTH: 03/09/2003

Left Watford at U16 level and headed south to sign for the Albion. A big, strong centre-half, he is comfortable on the ball and very good at defending one-v-one.

LEIGH KAVANAGH

POSITION: Centre Back
DATE OF BIRTH: 27/12/2003

Formerly with St Joseph's Boys in Ireland, he is another strong, comfortable, ball-playing centre-half. He is a leader on the pitch.

JOHN LUCERO

POSITION: Right Back
DATE OF BIRTH: 01/12/2003

Came into the club at under-12 level from Peacehaven. He is a good technician and a very good learner – a student of the game.

SAMY CHOUCHANE

POSITION: Centre Midfield
DATE OF BIRTH: 05/09/2003

Was picked up playing grassroots football in France and is a very combative ball-playing midfielder. Scored at the semi-final stage as Albion won the Premier League U17 Cup last season.

CASPER NILSSON

POSITION: Right Back
DATE OF BIRTH: 26/11/2003

Signed from Swedish club Malmo at U16 level, he has represented his country at U15 level and is a flying right-back who likes to get forward, but he can also defend.

ZAK STURGE

POSITION: Left Back
DATE OF BIRTH: 15/06/2004

A player who arrived from grassroots football late in the programme, he is a very adventurous and attack-minded left-back. He likes to join in with the play and is very athletic and quick.

JAAMI QURESHI

POSITION: Left / Right Wing
DATE OF BIRTH: 02/02/2004

A player who arrived at U11 level, he is a Surrey boy who is a tricky winger with good feet. He likes to show off his skills and can play anywhere across the front line.

1. MEGAN WALSH

POSITION Goalkeeper **DOB: 12/11/1994**

Bromsgrove-born Walsh started her career at Aston Villa prior to a move to Everton in 2013. Switches to Notts County and Yeovil Town followed before she joined Albion in July 2019. Walsh, who had been capped by England between U17 and U23 level, made 15 appearances during Albion's record-breaking 2020/21 FA WSL campaign, as they finished sixth – their highest-ever league position.

3. FLISS GIBBONS

POSITION: Defender **DOB: 09/07/1994**

Gibbons has plied her trade as both a defender and striker during her career. Having started out at Charlton Athletic and then Watford, the Maidstone-born player originally joined Albion back in 2014/15. Her ten goals in 17 appearances during the campaign saw her named Women's Player of the Year. Moves to Millwall and Gillingham followed. Gibbons returned to Albion in August 2017, after a season in which she netted 33 time in 19 appearances for the Gills.

5. DANIQUE KERKDIJK

POSITION Defender **DOB: 01/05/1996**

Dutch international Kerkdijk was part of the Netherlands squad that finished as runners-up at 2019 FIFA Women's World Cup. That same summer, she signed for Albion from Bristol City, having previously won three major trophies – including the Eredivisie – during her time with FC Twente. She made 23 appearances for Albion during the 2020/21 season and put pen-to-paper on a new one-year contract with the club in the summer of 2021.

2. EMMA KOIVISTO

POSITION: Defender **DOB: 25/09/1994**

Finnish international Koivisto has won over 50 caps for her country to date and was a member of the squad which secured qualification for the European Championships, which will be hosted in England in 2022. At club level, the versatile player – who is capable of playing in defence and midfield – won the Swedish top flight with BK Hacken (then known as Kopparbergs/Gothenburg FC) in 2020 prior to a move to Albion in February 2021 on an 18-month contract.

4. DANI BOWMAN

POSITION: Midfielder **DOB: 31/10/1988**

Club captain Bowman joined Albion in the summer of 2017 after spells with Arsenal, Chelsea and Notts County and was named the club's Women's Player of the Season in her debut campaign with the club. Able to operate in central defence or midfield, Bowman has made more than 40 WSL appearances for Albion, although her 2020/21 season was curtailed by a foot injury which required surgery. She has won nine caps for England.

6. MAYA LE TISSIER

POSITION: Defender **DOB: 18/04/2002**

Born in Guernsey, Le Tissier represents England at international level, with the defender having won caps for the Young Lions' U17 and U19 teams so far in her fledgling career. Having joined Albion in May 2018, she made her debut for the club against rivals Crystal Palace in a Continental Cup fixture in December 2018. She has made over 30 FA WSL appearances for Albion to date and signed a new contract with the club in September 2021.

7. AILEEN WHELAN

POSITION: Midfielder   **DOB:** 11/08/1991

Whelan has made over 70 appearances for Albion since signing for the club from Everton back in 2017. Able to play in either wide or central midfield or up front, she also turned out for the likes of MK Dons, Nottingham Forest and Notts County earlier in her career. The former England U23 international won the World Student Games as a member of Team GB in 2013 while away from football, she has a Master's degree in Applied Child Psychology.

9. GEUMMIN LEE

POSITION Forward   **DOB:** 07/04/1994

After her successful season on loan with Albion in 2020/21, the club were able to secure the services of South Korean international Lee on a permanent basis in the summer of 2021. She scored three goals in 18 FA WSL matches for the Seagulls last season, whilst on loan from Manchester City. She started the 2021/22 campaign in impressive form with goals in Albion's 2-0 home victory over West Ham and their 5-0 away win at Birmingham City.

8. MEGAN CONNOLLY

POSITION Midfielder   **DOB:** 07/03/1997

Cork-born Connolly arrived at Albion in January 2019 after playing college football in the United States with Florida State Seminoles. The Republic of Ireland international made her Seagulls debut against Manchester City that same month. A midfielder with an eye for goal, Connolly scored a Goal of the Season contender with a right-footed shot from outside the penalty area in the 2-0 win over Birmingham City on the opening weekend of the 2020/21 FA WSL campaign.

10. INESSA KAAGMAN

POSITION: Midfielder   **DOB:** 17/04/1996

Kaagman represented the Netherlands at the delayed 2020 Olympic Games in Japan in the summer of 2021 on the back of an impressive debut season with Albion. The Dutch midfielder netted nine times in 25 appearances in all competitions in 2020/21, ending the campaign as the Seagulls' top scorer. A two-time Eredivisie winner with Ajax, Kaagman scored ten goals in 41 appearances for Everton between 2018 and 2020 prior to joining Albion.

BRIGHTON & HOVE ALBION WOMEN

BRIGHTON & HOVE ALBION
WOMEN

11. RINSOLA BABAJIDE

POSITION Forward **DOB:** 17/06/1998

London-born Babajide joined Albion on a season-long loan from Liverpool in July 2021, making her club debut as a substitute in the 5-0 away win at Birmingham City in September 2021. Formerly of Crystal Palace, Millwall and Watford, She was named as Liverpool's Player of the Season in her debut campaign with the Reds in 2019/20. Previously, she was part of the England squad that finished third at the 2018 FIFA U20 World Cup.

15. KAYLEIGH GREEN

POSITION: Forward **DOB:** 22/03/1988

Capable of playing in midfield, up front or as a wing-back, Green joined Albion from Yeovil Town in the summer of 2018. She began her career with Cardiff City, where she made her European debut in the UEFA Women's Champions League, before moving to Yeovil in March 2016. She spent a loan spell with Italian club Chieti Calcio Femminile whilst under contract with Yeovil. The Welsh international has since featured in over 50 matches for Albion.

13 FRAN STENSON

POSITION: Goalkeeper **DOB:** 27/04/2001

Stenson bolstered Albion's goalkeeping options in the summer of 2021, joining the club on loan from Arsenal for the season. Having made her FA WSL debut during her time at Birmingham City, she signed for Manchester City in 2018. She was loaned to Blackburn Rovers during her time as a Citizen before she was on the move again in 2019, signing for Arsenal. She spent a second loan spell with Rovers in 2019/20, featuring in eight Championship games.

16. ELLIE BRAZIL

POSITION Forward **DOB:** 10/01/1999

A talented footballer and athlete, Brazil won gold in the 800 metres at the 2015 English Schools' Athletics Championships prior to joining Derby County's academy. Having made her senior breakthrough at Birmingham City, she signed for Italian side Fiorentina in August 2017, before returning to the UK in July 2018 to join Albion, for whom she has made over 40 senior appearances to date. Brazil was a regular in Hope Powell's starting XI in 2020/21.

18. DANIELLE CARTER
POSITION Forward **DOB:** 18/05/1993

A three-time FA Cup winner with Arsenal, Carter scored the winning goal in the 2016 final victory over Chelsea. The Solihull-born forward also won the FA WSL during her 11 years with the north London giants, for whom she made over a century of appearances. Carter, who has represented England at every age group from U17s to senior, joined Reading in July 2020 before signing for Albion a year later.

20. VICTORIA WILLIAMS
POSITION: Defender **DOB:** 08/08/2002

Having arrived on a free transfer from Sunderland back in July 2018, Williams has been a key member of Albion's first-team squad ever since. The defender spent time with Doncaster, Arsenal and Leeds as a youth player, making her debut for the latter in 2007. Spells with Doncaster Belles, Chelsea and Sunderland followed prior to her south coast move. Williams, who has captained Albion on a number of occasions, signed a new contract with the club in May 2021.

24. MAISIE SYMONDS
POSITION Midfielder **DOB:** 02/02/2003

Symonds joined Albion from Chelsea in January 2021 and featured in two FA WSL matches for the Seagulls before putting pen-to-paper on a contract with the club that summer. The U19 international made her FA WSL debut in a win over Bristol City in May 2021, before making her first professional start for Albion in the FA Women's Cup – a 6-0 win over Huddersfield Town on the final day of the season.

19. EMILY SIMPKINS
POSITION: Midfielder **DOB:** 25/05/1990

Simpkins became the first Doncaster Rovers Belles player to sign a professional contract back during her second spell with the club between 2015 and 2018. A past Leicester City, Nottingham Forest and Birmingham City player, she has featured in over 30 FA WSL matches for Albion since joining the club in August 2018. She signed a new one-year contract in June 2021.

22. KATIE ROBINSON
POSITION: Forward **DOB:** 08/08/2002

England U17 international Robinson joined Albion from Bristol City at the beginning of the 2020/21 season on the back of nearly 30 senior appearances for the Robins. Unfortunately, a knee injury soon after making her Seagulls debut against Birmingham City in September 2020 saw her ruled out for the remainder of the campaign. She returned to first-team action in the 5-0 thrashing of Birmingham in September 2021.

40. LIBBY BANCE
POSITION: Midfielder **DOB:** 23/07/2003

A graduate of Albion's youth academy, Bance made her senior professional debut in a League Cup match against London Bees in 2019 while her first FA WSL appearance came in a 1-0 win over West Ham in November 2020. Bance, who originally joined Albion as a 12-year-old, was invited to join an England U19 training camp in June 2021. Around the same time, she signed her first professional contract with the Seagulls, having made ten senior appearances in 2020/21.

PASCAL GROSS
AMEX HERO

Pascal Gross was Brighton's first signing ahead of their debut Premier League campaign in 2017/18. Now playing his fifth season with the Albion, Gross has become a real crowd favourite and a player whose presence at the club has become synonymous with the successful Premier League era that the Seagulls have enjoyed at the Amex Stadium.

Shrewdly recruited by then-Brighton boss Chris Hughton, Gross joined from German side Ingolstadt 04 with who he had made close to 200 appearances in the top two tiers of the Bundesliga, and was seen as Ingolstadt's stand-out player before joining the Seagulls.

Born in Mannheim, he began his career with Hoffenheim in 2008, before switching to Karlsruhe in 2011 and then moving to Ingolstadt in 2012.

He made his Albion debut in the club's opening Premier League fixture against Manchester City at the Amex Stadium, and went on to win the club's Player of the Season award after numerous impressive displays.

The German took the mantle of scoring the club's first-ever Premier League goal, against West Bromwich Albion, and also headed the all-important winning goal against Manchester United at the Amex, which secured the club's top-flight safety. Following that highly-successful maiden campaign for both club and player, Gross agreed a contract extension.

Gross was on target against Manchester United again the following August, scoring from the penalty spot in an unforgettable 3-2 win at the Amex.

He netted twice more during 2018/19, scoring in a 2-1 defeat to Manchester United at Old Trafford, before netting a crucial equaliser in a 1-1 draw with Newcastle United in April.

With the ability to operate as a creative spark in the centre of midfield or in a wide role, Gross has developed a reputation as an attack-minded player who has served the Seagulls superbly under the management of both Hughton and current head coach Graham Potter.

The 2019/20 season saw Gross feature in 29 of Albion's 38 Premier League games and his first goal of the season set the Seagulls en route to a vital 3-2 Amex victory over Everton in October 2019. His second goal of the campaign coincided with Glenn Murray's final goal for the club as Albion staged a thrilling comeback to take a share of the points following an eventful 3-3 draw with West Ham United at London Stadium.

Last season saw Gross make 40 first-team appearances in all competitions with the talented German on target in back-to-back home fixtures against Premier League champions Liverpool and south-coast rivals Southampton. He also kept his cool from the spot to open the scoring against Leeds United in May 2021 as Brighton recorded a Premier League double over the Yorkshire side.

Gross' contribution to the Seagulls' Premier League adventures certainly show no sign of letting up as he set up Alexis Mac Allister's winner at Burnley on the opening day of 2021/22.

FULL NAME:	Pascal Gross
DATE OF BIRTH:	15 June 1991
PLACE OF BIRTH:	Mannheim, Germany
POSITION:	Midfielder

SEAGULLS APPEARANCES	SEAGULLS GOALS
137	**15**
LEAGUE: *126*	LEAGUE: *15*
FA CUP: *6*	FA CUP: *0*
LEAGUE CUP: *5*	LEAGUE CUP: *0*

ALBION DEBUT: Brighton & Hove Albion 0-2 Manchester City
12 August 2017 · Premier League

ALBION HONOURS: Player of the Season 2017/18

APPEARANCE AND GOALS CORRECT AS AT JUNE 2021

GROSS NETS ALBION'S FIRST-EVER PREMIER LEAGUE GOAL

ANSWERS

50. REWIND QUIZ OF THE YEAR

1. Chelsea and West Bromwich Albion. **2.** Lech Posnan.
3. Leandro Trossard. **4.** Adam Lallana. **5.** Portsmouth.
6. Alexis Mac Allister. **7.** Newcastle United.
8. The eleventh attempt (defeating Tottenham Hotspur on
31 January 2021) **9.** 4-3. **10.** Wolverhampton Wanderers.
11. Swansea City. **12.** Aston Villa. **13.** Southampton.
14. 1982. **15.** True (Leicester City). **16.** Newcastle United
and Leeds United. **17.** Dan Burn. **18.** Four (Sanchez,
Ryan, Steele and Walton). **19.** 41 points. **20.** 12.

70. PREMIER LEAGUE QUIZ

1. 2006/07. **2.** Oli Watkins (from Brentford in 2020).
3. 1946/47. **4.** Brentford's new Community Stadium.
5. New Zealand. **6.** Anderlecht. **7.** Manchester City.
8. Michael Keane (v Montenegro). **9.** Eddie Gray (2004).
10. Two (Liverpool and Watford). **11.** Roma.
12. Sergio Aguero. **13.** Brandon Williams (Norwich City).
14. Eight goals. **15.** Alex Neil. **16.** Newcastle United.
17. Norwich City (on loan in 2012/13). **18.** Four
(Javi Gracia, Quique Flores, Hayden Mullins twice and
Nigel Pearson). **19.** Ian Wright. **20.** Matt Jarvis (in 2011).